Never Leave
Your Block

By Scott Jacobs

Copyright 2012 Scott Jacobs
First Edition

These articles originally appeared in *The Week Behind* and are reproduced
with both thanks and acknowledgment: www.theweekbehind.com

Library of Congress Cataloging-in-Publication Data
Jacobs, Scott, 1950 —

Never Leave Your Block
by Scott Jacobs

1. Social Sciences 2. Wit and Humor I. Title

ISBN: 1-879652-00-5
EAN13: 9781879652019

Designed by Jell Creative Inc., Chicago, IL. Printed in the United States.

www.deadtreepress.com

For Lucy

Table of Contents

Never Leave Your Block

When I was still living the life of a young reporter in Chicago In the early 1970s, I never grew tired of the surprises the city would throw at me. On the subway, I'd meet people with remarkable life stories; in the dark halls of public housing projects, I'd see acts of remarkable kindness; in the confines of City Hall, I was witness to bluster of histrionic proportion. I got into journalism with some vague notion that my words might somehow bring about more enlightened public policy. My years as a general assignment reporter, however, convinced me that enlightenment doesn't emanate from you. It comes to you by being open to experiencing the real lives of the people around you.

One night, for instance, I was sent out to cover a race riot in Marquette Park on Chicago's southwest side. In those days, my newspaper, *The Sun-Times*, was so cheap they sent me out to cover it on the subway and gave me two dimes to phone in my report. As my deadline approached, I ducked into a bar looking for a pay phone and found myself in "The Midget Club" — a bar designed and operated for Chicago's little people. All the bar stools were chopped down to midget size. There was a mural behind the bar of a scene from The Wizard of Oz, and the phone itself was only a few feet off the ground. After calling in my report, I forgot all about the riot and settled in to hear how Parnell St. Aubin, who played a Munchkin in the 1939 movie, and his wife Mary came to run the club. If only I could write about that, I thought.

In those days, the reporters in town gathered after work at a bar named Riccardo's on Rush Street. That is where I met Ed McCahill, a kid off the streets of Gage Park who worked his way up the journalistic ladder through

The City News Bureau to become editor of a prestigious urban planning journal at the University of Chicago. The journal featured learned essays on race, poverty, education and regional planning issues, but McCahill never fit the editor mold. "What does any of this mean to people in my neighborhood?" he would say. "You want to know what's going on in America? Never leave your block. Everything you need to know is right there. That's where the action is."

Not long after, Ed became disenchanted with the notion that journalism could change the world and quit his job. For one glorious summer, I followed him around his haunts in Old Town like Boswell tagging along behind Samuel Johnson. After breakfast at Nookies, he'd work his way down the street to Sam's hardware — where he'd pick up freelance carpentry work — and various places in between where Ed had eight or nine conversations going on at once with shopkeepers, doormen and parking lot attendants along the way.

Being half Irish and half Croatian, Ed had the gift of gab. People opened up to him like flowers after the first rainstorm in the spring. He had a laugh — an infectious laugh, both genuine and reassuring — that made people feel safe telling him their secrets. And he carried those secrets around with him day to day, building a database of human experience that none of those charts and studies he published in his scholarly journal could ever approach.

By Ed's estimation, the reason you live where you live is because you are comfortable living there. And comfort is not something pollsters can easily get at. It's a feeling, the sense that you live in a community where you are valued, where you value your neighbors, and your shared values are respected by and incorporated in the laws of the land. Out of this sense of comfort comes the American experience. Who you are, where you live, what happens in your life — all this comes into play when you try to place yourself in the American experience.

This is a book about one small neighborhood in Chicago that, in truth, exists in every city in America. My neighborhood goes by the name of Bucktown and it lies about 10 minutes from downtown on the northwest side of Chicago. I've chosen to write about it because that's where I live. By sharing my experiences there, I hope you will take a moment to look at your own neighborhood in the same light.

In case you are wondering, my old friend Ed never was one to take his own advice. A few years after our summer together, he left Chicago to follow his dreams. He went to live on a beach in Mexico for a few years, hired on as a construction worker in Las Vegas during the housing boom, then shipped out with the merchant marines to ports unknown in the Pacific. The last I heard, he was working as a security guard at a housing project in Hilo, Hawaii.

This book is dedicated to Ed. Because wherever he is, whatever he is doing, he taught me the fine art of listening.

A Garden in The City

A Long Walk Through My Neighborhood

A long walk through my neighborhood will take you past a muffler repair shop, two locksmiths, a neon sign store, an insurance agency, a day labor recruitment center (across from a bar) and a Puerto Rican flag stand — and that's only in the first block.

On my walk, I'll encounter half a dozen street vendors with pushcarts, kids swimming in a public pool, mechanics gathered around the undercarriage of a car, and teenagers churning elbows and hips in a never-ending game of alley basketball.

I can eat at Mexican, Cuban, Chinese, Argentinean and Italian restaurants or stop by the new Think Cafe serving something they call "Nouveau California." For all of its diversity, I walk my neighborhood with ease secure in the thought everyone has more important things to do than bother me.

I can hear Spanish and English in equal measure on street corners, attend church services conducted in Polish, Spanish and English, often at the same time, and catch hip hop and hard rock seeping from the headphones of teenagers standing at the bus stop.

Neighbors wave at me as they walk their dogs. Gardeners pause to mull with me the prospects of rain. The homeless push their grocery carts to the side when I come through my alley. The waitress at the corner diner knows my name — and what I will order. If there has ever been a better neighborhood than this, I don't know it because this neighborhood is mine. I chose it, or it chose me.

The day I moved in is so distant now I forget what brought me here. I remember driving around Chicago in the heat of July with a real estate agent following a trail of listing sheets, looking into other people's abodes, sniffing through their kitchens, prying into their closets and surveying their basements to assess the age and condition of their furnace.

The act of house hunting, which all of us practice at some point in our lives — and many practice over and over again — is meant to proceed along certain set parameters: price, location, needs and amenities. But there is another factor — a "comfort zone" — that always seems to emerge out of a mysterious sense of whether a neighborhood is right for you, and whether you are right for the neighborhood.

When I came upon my current house, there was nothing in the modest bungalow that told me, going in, this is the one. The wafting smell of Kentucky Fried Chicken from across the alley in back was strong, and the noise of the expressway — only half a block away — was blessedly weak. It is hard to say how exactly one decides that a house fits you, but on walking out, both my wife and I said, "This is the one." And soon enough, it was ours.

The community I moved into is called Bucktown, a flat, grassy piece of Chicago first staked out in 1854 in what was then the northwestern corner of the city. The first residents came from Germany, settling around a 3-acre park they called Holstein on streets named after familiar German landmarks and towns. Because they were known to keep goats in their front yards, their community was called, derisively, Bucktown.

In The Great Migration that flooded America with over 20 million European immigrants in the late 1800s, the railroads brought nearly one million of them to Chicago. Drawn by common language and customs, each gravitated to their own ethnic neighborhoods. The Germans stuck to Lincoln Park, the Irish to Bridgeport, Beverly and Austin, the Italians to the North Side and Taylor Street.

Those that came to Bucktown were predominantly Polish, settling first around the St. Stanislaus Kosta Cathedral at Noble and Evergreen, then drifting north along Milwaukee Avenue or southwest along Archer Avenue. By 1920, census takers would count over 280,000 Poles in Chicago. More than half of them lived in or near Bucktown. They were among the poorest of Chicago residents, packed 450 people to an acre, in bungalows, two-flats and tenements crammed against vaulted sidewalks and dirt filled streets. Not infrequently, families put two adults and six children in their 2-bedroom flats. The tri-corner park at Milwaukee, Division and Ashland was called "The Polish Downtown." But it was not a glitzy strip.

Census takers in 1880, 1890 and 1900 found more than 50 percent of the men in Bucktown listed their occupations as "common laborers." Only a handful listed themselves as professionals. In Poland, they'd been called chlopi, or peasants; and once in Chicago, they found themselves on the lowest rung of the social ladder. But what they lacked in money, they made up for in faith.

The three spires of St. Stan's, St. Hedwig's and St. Mary of The Angels still dominate the Bucktown skyline and hold within them the history of Bucktown and, in many ways, the history of Polish Catholics in America. All three were the handiwork of Father Vincent Michael Barzynski, the iron-willed pastor of St. Stan's who came to Chicago in 1874 just as the first wave of Polish immigrants were arriving.

Barzynski oversaw completion of St. Stan's in 1881, then seeded a new parish called St. Hedwig's on land he purchased a mile north at Webster and Hoyne in 1888. When parishioners out-numbered seats, he created yet another parish in 1899, St. Mary's of The Angels, at Hermitage and Cortland, right between the two.

Chicago Alderman Ed Burke writes in the introduction to *The Old Chicago Neighborhood* that each of these Chicago parishes defined neighborhood boundaries and became "shorthand identifications that quickly provided a host of social, cultural and economic statistics" about its residents.

"Nothing helped to civilize the variety of life across Chicago's neighborhoods more than the Roman Catholic Church," Burke writes. "The most intricate and intimate of life's comings and goings took place amid the rigors, rules and regimes of parish life. The story of parishes is the story of schools, gymnasiums, religious pageants and countless weddings, funerals and Sunday Masses. But it is also more. Woven into the lifecycle and heartbeat of parish life is the sustaining power of belonging and being home... Experiences were shared and convoked with a mutuality that lasted a lifetime. Parish ties were familiar and familial, providing a sense of turf and sacred space."

Of the three churches, St. Hedwig's most embodies the character of the neighborhood. The squat, stone cathedral was completed in 1901, but only barely — the domes on its twin towers were poured from concrete when construction funds ran out. In its early days, before the new church was finished, St. Hedwig's was the site of one of Bucktown's most historic events — the famous "Pepper Riots" of 1895.

Although it had been in existence for only six years, St. Hedwig's was then creaking under the pressures of thousands of new Polish immigrants coming into the neighborhood. Father Barzynski appointed his brother, Joseph Barzynski, to run the parish, but the burden of servicing 1300 parishioners led him to seek help from a younger pastor, only 25, named Anthony Koslowski.

Gary Hogan, a pastor at St. Hedwig's and the neighborhood historian, said the two got along like oil and water. Barzynski was set in his old fuddy-duddy ways while Koslowski was a young, charismatic, fiery orator who appealed to the young, new generation of Polish immigrants.

"Basically, it became a personality conflict," Hogan said, but it was a conflict that would create a schism in the neighborhood lasting almost 90 years. It was a classic fight in the immigrant experience. "The issues between them came down to what seems now an abstract point — are we Polish Catholics or Catholic Poles?" Hogan said. "Like a lot of ethnic groups, the Poles were still trying to figure out their role in America, how to blend in and still keep their culture. Barzynski said we are Poles living as Catholics in America, so we are American Catholics who follow the Pope in Rome. Koslowski said we are Polish Catholics who honor our country first, and our religion second. So the parish split into camps. There were protests out on the sidewalk and many attempts to take over the church during services. Finally, Barzynski barricaded himself in the church rectory, but Koslowski's followers stormed that too to throw him out."

Dubbing the incident "The Pepper Riots," *The Chicago Tribune* reported on February 7, 1895 that police were called to the St. Hedwig's rectory where 3,000 protestors gathered outside. The crowd broke into the foyer and assaulted the priests. When police intervened, the protestors threw red pepper into their eyes. Shots were fired and dozens were injured, including one policeman who was struck by a hammer.

Reading the *Tribune* account the next day, Chicago Archbishop Patrick Feehan closed down the church for nine months, trying to negotiate a truce between the two priests. Three times the church tried to re-open, and three times protestors blocked services.

By May, Koslowski decided to form his own church outside the control of the archdiocese. Taking 1000 of St. Hedwig's 1300-member congregation with him, he moved three blocks away to Charleston Street and built a fourth church, All Saints Cathedral. He called his new religious order The Polish National Catholic Church. Ex-communicated for this act, and without the financial support of Rome, Koslowski made a name for himself preaching Polish nationalism around the Midwest, but the All Saints cathedral never grew beyond its original base. It muddled along for a number of decades and, long after the dispute settled into the dust of history, the two factions reunited on the centennial anniversary of St. Hedwig's in 1988. All Saints was eventually sold a few years ago to a Presbyterian congregation seeking to build a new congregation among the yuppies moving into Bucktown.

But St. Hedwig's thrived. Bolstered by yet another wave of Polish immigration, it grew to become one of the largest parishes in Chicago with 3,746 families. The parish school, known as the St. Hedwig's Industrial School, taught classes in English and Polish and focused on providing basic vocational skills for factory-bound immigrants. In its heyday, just before World War II, the school served 2,259 students. It was as large as any public school in the city.

In the 1930s, 1940s and 1950s, Bucktown was the quintessential Chicago ward (the 32nd) run by the quintessential Democratic machine boss, Big Joe (Rusty) Rostenkowski. It was neither the city's most powerful or most benign, but a stalwart blue-collar neighborhood of solid Democratic values. His son Danny, the former Congressman from the district who rose to become chairman of the U.S. House Ways and Means Committee, remembered how his grandfather ran a savings and loan out of his basement across from St. Stan's and his father, the alderman, argued politics in local saloons while the children ran wild through the neighborhood.

"There was such community spirit," he recalled. "The park district used to come here and put a wooden sidewalk over the cement so that you could walk with your ice skates on the wood to go into the park to warm up or walk to the ice. They used to flood that park. I remember my mother bringing big urns of hot chocolate for all the kids when we were outside all day. You are talking about community spirit, and it was fantastic."

In the 1950s, Bucktown began changing. Not racially changing, as we sometimes think of it (but that would come), but physically changing. The chief instrument of that change would be the automobile.

For Bucktown, it was the harbinger of both increased mobility and imminent doom. At the end of World War II, with automobiles pouring off the assembly lines, and suburban developments blossoming on the city out-skirts, Chicagoans suddenly discovered opportunities to move, build new houses on wider lots and re-invent their lives in the suburbs.

The more affluent in the community began moving northwest. But for those left behind, the automobile was a double-edged sword. Automobiles required roads. More precisely, expressways and in 1955 Bucktown lay dead center in the path of the largest in the world, the Kennedy Expressway.

Older residents could see it coming. The corridor for a northwest super-highway into downtown Chicago had been designated as early as the 1930s. When a new Mayor Richard J. Daley signed the deal to annex land for a new O'Hare airport on the northwest corner of Chicago in 1955, the die was cast. In 1956, President Eisenhower pushed through Congress the Interstate Highway Act (the crowning achievement of his presidency, he later said), and one of Mayor Daley's first acts was to take advantage of the 90 percent federal matching funds to build an expressway connecting the airport to downtown.

The route for the Northwest Expressway (renamed The Kennedy shortly after Kennedy's assassination) cut through the northwest corner of St. Hedwig's parish. Hundreds of homes in its path were bulldozed, and only through the magic of Polish politics — something to do with the Morton Salt Company's desire to give up its salt yard in exchange for keeping the Chicago winter salt contract — was the expressway re-routed 300 feet east to prevent the demolition of St. Stan's itself.

By the time the expressway was completed in November 1960, St. Hedwig's was a shadow of its former self. "The expressway tore right through the heart of the community," Hogan said. "Every parish felt the impact. But we took the biggest hit."

School attendance at St. Hedwig's dropped to less than 750 students before it closed in 1959. The grand St. Mary of The Angels, which opened in 1920 as a Roman Renaissance tribute to St. Peter's Basilica in Rome, closed in 1988 because the archdiocese could not keep up with the repairs. But St. Stan's, the mother church, had been saved and, with Danny Rostenkowski now in Congress, slow improvements started to come to the neighborhood.

If you walk through my neighborhood, the signs of Bucktown's old German and Polish heritage are worn and faded. Streets once named Hamburg, Frankfort, Berlin, Koblentz and Bremen are gone, replaced in a wave of anti-German sentiment during World War I by new names that seem to be ripped from an English village map: Webster, Lyndale, Claremont, Shakespeare, and Medill (after the *Tribune* publisher) But there is another flavor in the air, a Latin flair that speaks to the next phase of Bucktown's life.

Geographically, Bucktown occupies slightly over one square mile just minutes from Chicago's downtown Loop. The 2000 census places the population at 16,167 in 12 census tracts bounded by Fullerton on the north, North Avenue on the south, Western Avenue to the west and The Chicago River on the east. About 10,825 of them are white, a mixture of old Poles who have stuck it out and new Yuppies moving in. But another 4,223 are Hispanic, mostly Puerto Ricans who came to Chicago in the early 1970s and Mexicans who flooded in during the 1980s. The rest are a mixture of Afro-Americans, Asians and what census takers invariably call "other."

Ten years earlier in the 1990 census, Puerto Ricans and Mexicans made up over 50 percent of Bucktown. The two-flats and three flats built by the Poles and the storefronts along Western, Fullerton, Ashland and North Avenues filled with new immigrants speaking Spanish. But the businesses stayed the same. Fortunately, the new immigrants were also Catholic, but the resources of the Chicago archdiocese were spread thin at the time. Although the churches remained open, many Catholic schools did not; and more and more of the children slipped into the Chicago public school system.

The older residents who remember Bucktown in those days recall it was a time when neighborhood gangs ruled the parks, drugs were available on every street corner, and a sort of hopeless ennui dragged down property values and spirits. Looking to put a positive spin on the change, St. Hedwig put out a Centennial Book in 1988 that concluded, "St. Hedwig's Parish was founded as a beacon of hope to frightened immigrants 100 years ago. Today, 100 years later, it stands as a beacon of hope to new immigrants and contemporary men and women who may have lost their way in a world of distractions."

It was in the early 1970s that I had my first Bucktown experience. Throwing my $1,000 in with some friends, we purchased an old mansion on Caton Place in 1974 for $20,000. The deed at the bank had NOT FINANCEABLE stamped on every loan document surrounding the purchase due to the condition of the neighborhood. And there were other drawbacks, among them El trains whizzing by our window 20 feet away. But we soon came to enjoy our bohemian lifestyle in a community where you walked the streets in pairs, sometimes with a gun for protection.

When we moved in, the old mansion was being used as a boarding house. Twelve Polish students lived there in four bedrooms, a library and living room, half of them sleeping on military cots. We set about restoring the house, scraping green stucco from the woodwork, stocking a backyard pond with gold fish, and holding grand dinners in the dining room to the accompaniment of Straus waltzes. Friends who huddled closer to the lake in Old Town and Lincoln Park rarely made it across the Halsted Street divide to visit. But we did, on occasion, throw backyard parties under the L tracks, and once enjoyed the company of our most famous neighbor, Nelson Algren, who spent most of the evening on the back porch growling about interlopers. When our friendship dissolved, we sold the house and moved away.

But other students and artists, looking for cheap housing close to downtown, began moving in. Starting in the eighties, they made loft spaces into studios, factories into homes and houses into workspaces. Young, mostly white and all Gen X, they turned bowling alleys into rock clubs, furniture stores into galleries along Milwaukee Avenue and taverns into "performance spaces."

`They brought their art, and their art brought commerce, and commerce brought money. So the rents began to rise, the rehabbers stepped in, then the developers, then finally the well-heeled — buying old homes for a quarter of a million dollars only to tear them down to build million dollar mansions. (For those who care, we sold our "mansion" in 1976 for $22,000. The last time it changed hands the asking price was $859,000.)

Father Hogan said the neighborhood today is going through a risky transformation. "In the old days, you had a Polish family with two adults in one room and six children sharing another. The Mexicans and Puerto Ricans came, and it was very much the same. It was great when the rehabbers arrived. One at a time, they'd fix up homes. Whole streets would change," he said. "Now it's all just tear downs for condos. Your typical new family in Bucktown is two adults and, maybe, one child. And when he grows older, they're gone. They only stay four or five years. So everything in the parish is transient. People aren't setting down roots."

Mary Strong, who has lived in Bucktown for 43 years, is encouraged by the influx of new blood, but frightened by the tendency of developers to buy old bungalows only to replace them with million dollar homes "They're tearing down all the buildings. You go out in the morning and you don't know if the house next to you is going to be there when you get back at night," she says.

I have walked full circle now around Bucktown feeling like I am exploring some piece of gnarly bark wrapped around the very pulp of our city. Some parts of my neighborhood are so shiny bright I walk fast to get past them. Others draw my eye into a dark corner where, in a little garden, I smile to see a plastic chipmunk next to an American flag. St. Mary's stands gleaming in the sun. A five-year campaign by neighbors convinced the archdiocese to refurbish and re-open the church in 1998. A parish grade school and new day care center bustle with the sounds of children playing.

My path takes me up Damen past restaurants called Meritage, Absinthe and Confusion; and designer boutiques with names like Saffron, Tangerine and Kachi Bachi. Turning again, I find myself in Holstein Park where a hand-painted sign on the fence advertises the upcoming Bucktown Arts Fest, now in its 18th year.

Maria Mariottini, a graphic artist who took over the Arts Fest in the late 80s, is coming up the walk with her dog on a leash. This year will be the best ever, she says, with 170 booths scattered along the pathways of the park.

"It's really the best time of year," she says. "Everyone pitches in to help. My only fear with all the yuppies moving in is they're going to try to kick us out. They shouldn't move here if they don't want to live here. And if they don't like what we're doing, they can move out — which they'll probably do anyway."

There's a hint of conflict in the air. A foreboding that somehow, with the pressures of development, the center cannot hold. But life in Bucktown has always been that way. That's what happens when you fill a city with people.

— December 12, 2003

Basketballs & Ice Cream

Over the summer, I've begun to discover in this thicket of a neighborhood we inhabit where the kids like to hang out: my stoop.

Jorge and Jaime and Luis live just next door in a the third floor walk-up; Pete, Chris, Nick and Chris's sister, Cathie, have houses across the way; my own boys, Justin and Ben, also come in for the summer; and when Luis's buddies — an ever changing group of friends from high school — come over, the gang is pretty much up to full strength.

My stoop midway down the street is the perfect spot to kind of stand around and say, "Hey, what do you want to do next?" But it is not the only place. There is the Northwestern Bank parking lot for street hockey and baseball games (if you don't mind playing left field in the middle of Western Avenue), the alley behind Nick's for fireworks, and Margie's Candies for ice cream. There is also Holstein Park, which has a great pool and basketball court, but it lies in gang territory, according to Luis's mother. So no one is allowed to go there.

One thing that always seemed missing was a hoop — a basketball hoop.

Since I have an alley and a garage, I decided to go down to Sports Authority the other day to get one and, with a little help from the boys, put it up. It was well worth it. Over the summer, I watched the movement of the kids shift from stoop to alley, drawn by that beacon of hanging out — the hoop.

Sometimes, they'd come in waves. First Luis, Pete, Justin, Cathie — the older ones, all 14 to 16 years of age — "just shooting and hanging." Then the younger ones, Jorge, Ben, Jaime and Nick, 9 to 12, fresh from a water balloon fight looking to burn more energy. Or all at once, like some tom tom in the neighborhood beat out a secret rhythm saying, "Let's all go to the alley hoop and see who else is there."

Occasionally, I'd hear, and then see, a grudge match at the alley hoop: two fellas settling their differences with a free throw contest. More than once, I'd return home from work to find the youngest in the pack, Jorge, 9, just standing by the garage dribbling by himself waiting for me to take him on "one on one."

The best games were those that took place in the twilight before darkness. The twilight games were an ever-changing array of four-on-four match-ups playing to 6, 16 or 21 points. The teams were determined by recent grudges, current loyalties and who had to go to dinner; but all were, remarkably, age-balanced. At night, the orange fluorescent lights come on in the alley so it is no problem playing 'til 10 or 11 o'clock every night — and they did, frequently.

Whenever I'd go out to watch, I'd see this frantic flaying of elbows and off to the side, standing alone in the corner, Carlos, the silent one. Nobody will ever call Carlos thin, and shy doesn't begin to describe him. Carlos is one of Luis's buddies, the most respectful person you'd ever want to meet, who laughs at everyone's jokes but never seems to tell one.

I began to wonder one night whether Carlos was not playing because the other kids wouldn't pick him.

"Don't you want to get in there?" I asked.

"No, I just like to watch," he said.

Thereafter, I called Carlos The Watcher.

By summer's end, I knew we needed something to celebrate on the block. The 4th of July fireworks in the alley were a big hit, but when Mr. Diaz blew off the 1/4 stick of dynamite, my wife and I decided to look for a tamer form of recreation and organized the 1st Annual Medill Basketball Tournament & Ice Cream Social.

We determined there would be three contests you could win: Free Throws, Around the World and Coolest Lay-up. To make matters fair, there would be two divisions — over 13 and under 13 — with prizes including $50 gift certificates at Sports Authority, $15 gift certificates at Barnes & Noble and $5 gift certificates to Margie's Candies & Ice Cream Parlor for all who entered.

The day of the tournament was overcast. Most of the kids went to McFetridge Park for indoor skating in the morning and it was 4 or 5 o'clock before the first participants straggled in. Mike and Amy, visiting their uncle across the alley, wandered down asking if they could play. Soon enough, we had a quorum.

Around the World — a six-point game with a point for every basket you make from the three-point line — went easily to Luis (in the over 13 bracket) and Nick (in the under 13.) Young Ben won the Coolest Lay-up Contest with a bounce off the back of the factory wall, double pump, eyes-closed Hail Mary shot that miraculously went in.

When it was time for the Free Throw Contest, Nick swept the under-13 bracket again with 6 of 10 sinkers. In the over 13 category, this event normally belongs to Chris, 14, but he could only muster 3 hitters. Luis was hardly better with 4, followed by Mike, 4, and Amy, 2.

"Hey, Carlos, give it a try," I yelled.

"No thank you," he said.

"You have to," I shouted. "You can't be here without trying."

Carlos stepped to the line and, in the limpest of lame efforts, tossed the ball with his left hand at the hoop. It bounced from one side of the rim to the other, then fell in. Then he did it again, and again. Who knew Carlos was left-handed? He tossed up three more clunkers before he nailed another one.

With three shots to go, Carlos needed only one more to win. In the sports pages, you might say a hush fell over the crowd. But it didn't.

"You go, Carlos!" Luis shouted, twirling another ball between his legs and tossing a fist in the air.

"Carlos, my man!" Jaime said. "One more. You do it!"

The lines on Carlos face suddenly drew taut. He focused, and thought, and threw up another shot that clanged off to the side. His 9th shot clanged iron to the other side.

On the sidelines, the kids drew into a semi-circle around the hoop. Carlos set and delivered, and the ball swooshed through the hoop.

They laughed. They danced. They celebrated Carlos's achievements with fist slaps and high fives. This was truly a group of neighborhood kids who enjoy each other's company. They look out for each other. They will guard each other's secrets, but tell on a friend if they feel their friend did wrong. They care about each other. They stick together. They are a gang. The good kind. The kind that recognizes we are all in this together.

—August 15, 1998

Hector and Joe

If you want to get a haircut in my neighborhood, you have two choices — in the same block. There is Hector and there is Joe, once partners, who have divided up the 2600 block of West Fullerton in the most ecumenical way, by congregation.

Joe Vacarella, 57, is the proprietor of Joe's Barbershop, a two-seat affair in a little gingerbread storefront he has occupied for 18 years. Hector, his protégé for four of those years, is the owner of the 5-chair Hector's Barbershop just up the road.

In Hector's establishment, life is a party. Salsa music blares out of a CD player on the counter. A widescreen TV in back carries the latest DVD movies, and clients who are not actually getting haircuts wander from station to station offering style and design tips to those who are. Jose Munoz, a laid off county employee working on commission under neon clocks and illuminated posters for Pepsi and Mountain Dew, says he specializes in scissors and blow dry cuts. A barber known only as Kato works exclusively carving designs on Latin heads. He hands out a card after each saying, "I got faded at Hector's."

Some 20 years younger than Joe, Hector is known for his rapport with the local teenagers, especially the young Puerto Ricans who favor buzz cuts and skims. One recently gave him a new graffiti-style wall mural. He let another put a sign in his window promising, in addition to haircuts, "We Now Do Graphics." If you are young and looking for a hip place to hang, Hector's is your place.

Joe's is a decidedly more low-key situation. For Joe, cutting hair isn't a marketing opportunity, or even a business. It's a lifestyle, the only one he's known. His family hails from Foggia, a province on the Adriatic Sea, near the heel of Italy's boot. They owned a farm that stretched down to the seashore; but when his father, also a barber, saw a chance to come to America, he brought over the whole family to Chicago in 1955 when Joe was nine years old.

They moved into the Italian neighborhood around Taylor Street. Joe went to a procession of Chicago public schools, learning English on the streets of Little Italy, fighting his way through black gangs at Crane, and finally graduating from Austin High in 1964. He learned to cut hair at the age of 14 and joined his father three years later in a small shop just around the corner on California Street.

When you enter Joe's today, there is the feeling of a world that stopped somewhere around 1974. The walls are graced with a fading team picture of the 1969 Cubs, Dean Martin and Frank Sinatra in their prime, and a young Rocky Marciano, gloves poised, in his famous poster stance. An 8-track cassette player is playing Mantovani. ("I love Mantovani," Joe says, "The only thing I love more than Mantovani is 8-track cassettes. Best sound ever. I fix 'em, you know.") There's a mounted fish on the wall, skins from various prey Joe has hunted as an American Woodsman (see the official membership certificate) and a picture of Joe holding grapes and zucchini from his garden. Depending on the season, he will sometimes bring some in from his house in Park Ridge to give to his customers.

As low key as Joe's place is, it is always busy. "I work here ten, fourteen hours a day, seven days a week," Joe boasts. "I'm going to work here until I'm 101, and when I get too old to drive, I'm going to sell my house and move in upstairs." After a recent price hike, Joe charges $11 a head. Enough, he says, to get by.

When I went in for a haircut one recent Saturday, Joe had one in the chair and two more waiting in the wings. His regular assistant, Helen, was off for the day. The man in the chair was OJ. He was getting one of Joe's famous flat tops, just as he has every week for the last 24 years, and Joe was sharing with him the story of the 400-pound customer who broke his chair last week.

"Can you believe it, he busted the arms right off!" Joe said. "I asked him to slide back a little so he grabs the arms and, damned if the metal didn't snap right in two."

"That's your fault, you know," OJ said. "You need a bigger chair."

"A bigger chair? They don't even make these chairs anymore. Fortunately, another one of my customers is a welder and he was here that day. He put it back together, but we had to change the bolts."

"You know they had this same problem at McDonald's. Fat people couldn't fit in the booths so they had to get all new booths — so they weren't discriminating against fat people."

Joe snipped and buzzed in silence. "I'm not McDonald's," he said.

Joe saw me pawing through his magazines looking for something to read.

"I got a lot of new books this week. Here, try this one." He handed me a copy of Maxim. I glanced at the cover — "How to Get Her to Go Wild!" — and set it back on the pile. "It's not like Playboy. It's clean," Joe said. "But I got Playboy if you want it."

"I get lots of books. I signed up once for one magazine and I guess they sold my name to one of those companies who sell lists. So I get all these offers of free magazines. They send me a bill after 10 issues or so. I just write cancel on it and send it back. But I keep getting more and more books. I guess they think barbershops are good places to sell their book — and it's true. A lot of guys take the cards out and subscribe."

The stack beside me indeed had a lot of "books." *Automotive Parts, Mountain Bike, Maxim, Sporting News, Spin, Vibe, Inc, Penthouse, Men's Journal.*

"I don't have time to read them all. I just let them sit around, then I give 'em away."

Al, the postman, pokes his head in the doorway.

"Not today, huh?" he quickly surmises and leaves.

OJ steps out of the chair and another customer, a young Puerto Rican no more than 14 or 15, steps in. He tells Joe he wants "a bottle cap" — a popular cut not unlike the flat top Joe still favors, but more severe. Joe sizes up his head, then rips the electric clippers skintight up his back and neck, leveling off the top and painstakingly, hair by hair, feathering the edges together.

Joe is not a scissors man. He's got three or four electric clippers and he uses them all to get as close to the scalp as possible (without nipping the skin).

Joe's buddy Ray comes in the door carrying a six-pack of Miller's. Joe frowns. There are children in the chair. A big, hulking figure with a face out of the Soprano's, Ray goes immediately to the broom closet, drops the beer in a cooler and sits on a chair staring at Joe.

"You know where to get a good sub around here?" Joe asks. A customer offers that there's a submarine shop up on Addison. "You want a sub, Ray? I'm buying."

"You wanna a what?"

"A good sub. I need some food. You wanna go?" Ray gets up quietly.

"Any special kind? "

"A good Italian sub," Joe says. Ray leaves. Joe seems relieved.

Then Vic pokes his head into the doorway. He points to a slowly dripping air-conditioner that has left a puddle on the floor. "You know, you gotta fix this. Someone could slip," he says.

"So fix it," Joe says. "Aw, never mind. How are you doing?"

Vic takes that to be an invitation to enter and takes a chair near the window. He flips on the TV. The local news is reporting on the forest fires out west.

"You know, once half this earth was covered with fires — 135 million years ago," Joe opines to no one in particular. "It's true. An asteroid fell into the ocean in the Gulf of Mexico and everything got all disrupted and half the globe burned."

"Oh, you're full of shit," Vic says.

"It's true. 135 million years ago. Helen was there. She took pictures," Joe laughs.

"135 million years? That was before people. There was nothing before people, nothing we know of," Vic says.

"They got rocks, they got dinosaur bones," Joe says. "It's all in there. The scientists are pulling it out. Did you see that tape we got here? *A Walk with The Dinosaurs*? Beautiful tape, three and a half hours. It tells the whole story."

"You're crazy. That was before Jesus Christ. There was nothing before Jesus Christ."

"Vic, you gotta open your mind. Watch more television," Joe says.

When the boy is finished, it is my turn. I step into the chair. Joe asks what I want.

I respond not with a name, but a confession. "I haven't had it cut in about six weeks," I say.

"So shorter," Joe says, "but not too short."

"Yeah, exactly," I say. As he settles in to do his business, Joe scours his memory to get a fix on me. I've been in the shop four or five times before, but he can't place me.

"So what do you do?" he asks. I tell him I'm a writer. It seems to open a floodgate.

"I got a million stories," Joe says "Wait until my book comes out!"

"Are you writing a book?" I ask.

"Not exactly. In my mind, I got a million stories. Like my neighbor. I say 'hey, maybe you should cut your grass' and he says, 'you cut it. You're the barber,' and I say, "I don't do lawns!" And that's just the start. But I need a guy like you to write these down."

Someone asks Joe if he is going to be serving his homemade wine again this year at Christmas. "Just finished making it last week," he says. "I got 27 cases. I think that should be enough."

Wine making is another hobby Joe shared with his father. Every year in the middle of September, he goes down to the rail yards at 35th and Racine where brokers bring in boxcars of grapes from California and Michigan. They sell the wine grapes right off the boxcars parked on the sidings.

"There'll be 10, 15, maybe 20 boxcars. And they'll have a crate open and a sign telling you what kind of grape it is. You taste it, you like it, you buy it. You don't, you go to the next one."

"They're edible grapes, but they're not perfect grapes. You know, like some might be smaller, but they're still good. That's why they call them wine grapes."

I ask Joe how he makes his wine. He was waiting for this one. "First you stomp on them for about six months, then you wash your feet and you're done." He laughs. "I tell people that and, can you believe it, they buy it."

"But really, we got machines now," he continues. "What you do is you take the grape and, like, you break it. You don't crush it, and everything drops through the machine into the barrel. Then it sits for between three and ten days. Me, I do it Sunday to Sunday. After that, you strain it and put it in the main barrel. But you got to filter it. Otherwise you get residue."

"How do you know if you have a good batch", I ask.

"You taste it. If it's a little bitter, you might add a touch of sugar. But the most I ever used was five pounds for 55 gallons. That's like nothing."

Joe snips around the edges of my ear, then goes for the mirror.

"Do you do this with your kids?" I ask.

"They don't do it. They don't even like wine," Joe says. "The fact is it's a smelly process. You get those stains on the floor, on the wall, and the smell never goes away. Plus it's a lot of process, then a lot of cleaning and putting away stuff. But I enjoy it. I like the idea of taking something and making something else out of it...Want me to get those eyebrows?"

"First thing people see when they look you in the eye are those eyebrows. One's going up, one down, one sideways. They're like nose hairs. When people look at you, they're not looking at your face. They're looking at those weird eyebrows."

Joe clips my eyebrows, a sign that the masterwork nears its end. He reaches back for his Lux 400 to vacuum the stray hairs off my face and neck. "There, now that's a haircut," he says, "What's it been? Three months?"

"Something like that," I say and hand him my money.

"Say hello to the family," Joe says.

On my way home, I have to pass by Hector's. He is out front pitching pennies at a crack in the sidewalk with a couple friends.

"So did you get a good cut?" he asks.

I nod.

"Yeah, Joe always gives a good cut."

— October 17, 2003

The Rat Hunter

My neighbor — let's call him Dickon — has a thing for rats, the same thing American presidents seem to have for Osama bin Laden. Except Dickon once spent time in the U.S. Army Special Forces so he is far better equipped to act on it.

Every year about this time, he maps out an elaborate campaign to rid our block of the vile vermin. He starts by posting signs in the alley telling neighbors to keep their garbage bin lids closed. He reminds all the dog owners to clean up after their pet and generally police the area, an expression he picked up from his Army days. He calls the alderman demanding a "rat patrol" clean-up crew from Streets and Sanitation. But when they come, spreading their poison pellets by hand from plastic buckets, he scoffs at them like they are some kind of Cub Scout patrol lost on their way to Earth Day.

For Dickon, poison pellets are no more effective than trying to put out a fire with an eyedropper. Standard rattraps and cages are only slightly better. And that silly high-pitch sound machine I brought back from Home Depot one day? The only thing that scared away was my dog, he told me.

Rats are a wily breed, Dickon notes, far more suited to survive in an urban environment than we are. They can live in warm climes and cold, burrow through cement cracks as narrow as an inch to create nests and tunnels, feed off all manner of human waste, and use it to fuel a year round breeding frenzy.

A rat lives, on average, about three years. But young rats reach sexual maturity after three months; and when they do, it's Katy, bar the door. The females are capable of having as many as five litters a year, with up to 10

29

pups per litter. So chances are if you see one rat, you have not seen them all.

I've watched Dickon deploy a number of gadgets to eradicate the pests, everything from an electric Rat Zapper to Rodent's Revenge. The most ingenious was the African bucket trap developed by Zimbabwe wheat farmers to protect their crops.

To make the trap you need a 20-litre bucket, an ear of corn and a thick wire. Once you cut off the ends of the corn, you push the wire through it lengthwise, making sure the corncob can spin freely at the center of the wire. Bury the bucket in the ground, then fill it about 1/5th full of water. Bend the wire and push the ends firmly in the ground.

Every evening, coat the corn with peanut butter, then watch the rats climb out to get it and drop into the water. Remove the drowned rats in the morning. Using this device, Dickon once claimed he trapped 20 rats in a single week.

One morning, I walked out on the back porch to find Dickon taking the war to the rats under another neighbor's garage. He cut away all the weeds to reveal four gaping rat holes. He dug a 6" trench to wrap chicken wire around all sides of the garage, then poured a new layer of concrete over that. "That'll stop the bastards," he said. It didn't.

About a year ago, Dickon moved with his wife and two children to the suburbs, effectively abandoning the territory to the rodent Talibans. The other night, they came back for dinner and the first thing Dickon did was step out on the back porch to look out over the battlefield.

"How are the rats?" he asked.

I had to admit we'd lost a lot of ground. The rat holes were back under Elaine's garage. Just the night before, I said, I'd seen one scurrying across under my headlights as I turned into the alley. The rat stopped, turned and looked at me like I was the interloper not him.

"I've found the ultimate weapon," Dickon said triumphantly. "The Rodenator. It's a cross between a garden hose and a flame-thrower. You ought to get one."

The next day, I looked it up on the Internet. The Rodenator is the invention of an Idaho rancher named Ed Meyer. It was designed to eliminate gophers, badgers, prairie dogs, rabbits and other burrowing farm animals — rats being, in Dickon's mind, simply an urban manifestation of same.

The Rodenator operates on a mixture of oxygen and propane that is pumped into the burrow for approximately a minute then ignited with a single spark. The explosion is minimal, but the concussive force is enough to kill 92 percent of the animals in its path ("instantly and humanely," Meyer claims.) Failing that, it will nonetheless collapse the tunnel system so it's of little use to the rats or anyone else.

According to Meyer, the system is EPA-approved because it leaves no chemical residue in the ground. It also comes with a money-back guarantee if it does not work as advertised. But there is one little drawback. The base unit costs $2,000, not including the accessories and supplies that make it functional.

I have many neighbors on my block who have purchased snowblowers and generously clear our sidewalk in the winter. Maybe this summer, it's my turn to give back to the community. Maybe I should buy The Rodenator, strap on the ear protectors and go up and down the alley offering to blow up their garages. That'll show the bastards.

— May 13, 2009

The Bus to Horseshoe Heaven

The bus is parked on the sidewalk next to the Holstein Park field house. It's early morning, but that's no problem. The sign on the back of the bus announces the Horseshoe Casino Express runs 24 hours a day. And it's a good thing since the ladies of the Bucktown Seniors Club are lined up at 8 AM ready to go.

The occasion today is Dorothy Majewski's 82nd birthday. When the club saw the date approaching on the calendar, they gave her a choice: a luncheon at a nice restaurant or a gambling trip to the Horseshoe Casino in Hammond. It didn't take Dorothy but a split second to decide, and inside of two hours 25 other ladies had signed up to accompany her.

Gambling junkets are one of the favorite activities of The Bucktown Seniors Club. With free bus service from the Horseshoe Casino, they go down four times a year as a group. In smaller numbers, they go as frequently as once a week.

"I go almost every Sunday," says Florence Sokolowski. "I know the bus driver for the Trump Casino and, if I call him, he'll come by and pick me up right at my house. I stand by the curb and my neighbors think I'm waiting for the church bus. What do they know? But I might as well be going to church. People do more praying in a casino than they do in church, that's for sure."

Most of the women on the Horseshoe Casino bus carry with them their own Members Circle cards. The cards are free and, when you insert them into the slot machines, you can run up points for free merchandise — and the casino can track your gambling habits. The best thing about having a card, the seniors say, is that it allows you to enjoy discounted breakfast and lunch buffets. With the card, the all-you-can-eat breakfast is only $3.18 "and the Horseshoe has the best food of all the casinos," Dorothy claims.

On the way down to Indiana, I asked the seniors what games they like to play. All are slot machine players. Not a one likes to play the gaming tables. "I'm not a card player, " Mickey Kolasa says. "I went to the craps table once. That's the one with the 7 and 11, or whatever they holler out. But I'm always afraid of the other players because I think I'm holding up the game for them. So I just play the slots."

The Bucktown Seniors break down into three kinds of slot players: dollar, quarter and nickel. "The trick is to lose money as slow as you can," says Francis Stone. "I'd love to play the $1 slots, but if you put in your $50 and don't win, all your money's gone in 15 minutes and you're sitting around for an hour and a half with nothing to do."

Not everyone on the bus comes away a loser. Francis rode down to the Horseshoe next to Eleanor Turay, whom everyone calls "The Nickel Queen." Last time they all came down, Eleanor went off at the last minute to play the nickel slots and came away with an $800 jackpot.

"It was really only $700. The first $100 was what you might call my investment," Eleanor tells me. "But if you win big, these girls never let you forget."

The Horseshoe Casino is just over the Indiana state line. The bus turns off at the first exit after The Skyway, loops around a huge Horseshoe Casino sign as big as any in Las Vegas, and falls in behind another Horseshoe Casino bus — holding another club of octogenarians — to a VIP reception area only steps from the casino.

"This is where we come to deposit our grandchildren's inheritance," Eleanor jokes as she climbs off. But no one laughs. They are all gauging how much each plans to wager and/or is willing to lose.

In Indiana, and indeed most of the Midwest, gambling is only allowed on riverboats. It is a quaint conceit, based on the notion that riverboat gambling along The Mississippi River took place on paddleboats that were part of our heritage, and thus a tourist attraction.

Although the gambling halls of the Horseshoe Casino are, indeed, located in a boat that sits on water, they are about one-half of an inch away from land. Three hallway entrances seamlessly connect the gambling machines to the bars, restaurants, hotels and parking structures that make up the bulk of the enterprise. Were any of these boats ever to leave port, it would be like an earthquake through the center of San Francisco.

Which is to say, the Horseshoe Casino is one seamless gambling experience. Once the seniors step on board, they disperse themselves among the four floors of slot machines available for their use and pleasure.

I'm baffled by the array of new games available, and the many ways the casino has turned a nickel or quarter machine — at the press of a button — into a $2 or $5 wager. Fortunately, Josephine Dziminski, 85, comes to my rescue. Josephine is not only an old hand at the Horseshoe, one of her sons is a pit boss at the Bellagio in Las Vegas. Another is a lawyer with the Horseshoe organization. Josephine has gambled in casinos from Oncida, Wisconsin, to Bettancourt, Iowa, and she has one piece of advice. "Find a machine that works for you, then stay with it."

The Bucktown Seniors like to end their gambling junket around 1 PM so everyone can get home in time for their afternoon nap. They start gathering in the reception hall around 12:45 waiting for their bus to go home. As we wait, I notice bus after bus of new seniors still arriving.

For all the glamour associated with Las Vegas, gambling in Indiana appears to be a senior citizens sport. The ratio of 80-year-olds to 21-year-olds on the floor this Friday morning appears to be about 7 to 1.

When we climb back on the bus headed to Bucktown, Alice Bender, the senior coordinator, takes a head count to make sure everyone is on board.

"Now don't anybody fall asleep on the way back," she says. "One time, I left one of my members sleeping in the back of the bus. Everyone else got off at Holstein Park. But she slept her way right back to the casino."

— July 1, 2005

The Egg Hunt

The arrival of spring is greeted in our neighborhood by many religious ceremonies, Passover and Easter being the most prominent, but my favorite is the annual Holstein Park Egg Hunt, which marks the return of bedlam to Bucktown.

The sight of 150 preschool kids swarming across the dirt mounds of Senior Citizens Park is a harbinger of warmer days ahead — of t-ball tournaments, amoeba soccer games and a hundred heads bobbing in the Holstein pool.

Months of pent up energy, wasted on TV watching in days too cold to go out, explode in outdoor activity. And I'm not talking about the kids. I'm talking about the parents, coming out of winter hibernation for the first time to greet the neighbors and relearn the names of the other kids on the block.

The simplicity of holding an egg hunt should not be underestimated. Eggs are hidden and eggs are found. If you run out of eggs, the finder becomes a hider and you go all over again. Parents take pictures. Clothes get dirty. If the Park District smiles on you, you get the bunny costume for endless photo opportunities.

I know there are some who think the community would be better served by a more organized event. If everyone would just sign up in advance, form lines and follow instructions, we would never run out of eggs and all the children would have an equal chance to enjoy the day. As long as we've been doing this, however, I've never heard a kid complain and I'm always amazed how satisfied parents are just to get the family out and about on the first nice day of spring.

This is the sixth year we have been holding an egg hunt in Holstein Park, but the rules of engagement are always the same. One parent is responsible for showing up at 9 AM to clean up dog poop and hide the eggs; the other is responsible for bringing the kid later to collect them. (In the old days, we used to say 'fathers at 9, mothers at 10' but no one wants to be politically incorrect on the Internet.)

On the Friends of Holstein Park website, parents are asked to sign up for a 10 or 10:30 AM start time. One mother, a lawyer with two children, emailed me frantic that she had not signed up in advance. "Come anyway," I wrote back, "We only have rules to give the illusion of organization."

The time and date for the event, as well as the rules, are distributed in a monthly email called "Holstein Happenings." That alone is usually enough to guarantee a good turnout. This year, however, the *Sun-Times* picked up on it and listed Holstein first among a dozen free egg hunts last Saturday, so the crowd was bigger than ever.

The beauty of an egg hunt is that most of the kids don't know what they are celebrating. They come to chase their friends, dig in the dirt and get their picture taken. If they timidly hold back at the starting line, parents will gently prod them to show courage and move forward. If they gather too many eggs, it becomes a teaching moment about sharing.

From a kid perspective, think about it, what is the point of an egg hunt? Scattered out on the lawn are a bunch of multi-colored plastic ovals you are supposed to pick up before someone else does. Some are said to contain candy, but half the kids don't know yet what candy is. There are no prizes for collecting too many, or too few, or gold, silver and bronze ones. Your only reward is getting your picture taken with a park worker in a rabbit costume that looks like it was locked in a closet at Chuckie Cheese for the last year.

And yet, everyone leaves happy. Because at that age, any time you can spend with your parents is better than time without.

—April 1, 2010

The Virgin Under The Viaduct

There was more than a little excitement in the neighborhood last week after Obdulia Delgato found the image of the Virgin Mary in a water stain under the Kennedy Expressway.

Delgado, 31, had been driving by the spot for years but somehow last Sunday she glanced across an accident investigation site under the Fullerton exit and stopped dead in her tracks. There she saw in the seepage of salt water through cracks in the concrete the very image of the Virgin Mary. Her first instinct was to show her friends and family, which she did. Her second was to call the TV stations.

The first station she called was Univision, the Spanish-language station in Chicago, but no one there understood the import of her finding. Then she called NBC's Channel 5, where an enterprising assignment editor, looking at a blank slate for the Monday morning newscast after a slow weekend, quickly grasped the importance and sent out a crew.

The crowds started coming almost immediately. First it was a few curious neighbors drawn in by the NBC truck. Once other TV news operations picked up the story, a couple onlookers became a couple dozen, then a couple hundred, some coming in from distant suburbs to rub the spot. By the end of the week, the number of visitors amounted to several thousand.

The image Delgato saw was about five feet high and runs along a crack in the concrete holding up the freeway overhead. Dripping water from the expressway, heavily salted in the winter, has stained the grey area near the crack a lighter shade of grey. From a certain perspective — and especially at the low resolutions of a cellphone camera — the outline of the stain looks to have eyes staring out of a hood and two hands holding in prayer some rosary beads — next to which someone added the graffiti "Go Cubs."

By the time I got to the site early on the first morning, three candles and two flowers had been placed at the feet of the Mary. By nightfall, there were dozens of candles, police barriers holding back the crowd, groups praying in circles, and a flyer pasted on the wall advertising a conference of Hispanic Catholics.

I stood next to a woman who fancied herself something of an expert on Virgin Mary stains. A few months ago, she'd seen the grease stain Mary in the roadway down in Clearwater, Florida, and she'd heard just recently they were selling a piece of toast with the Virgin Mary's face in it on eBay (although she did not bid). This Mary is better formed than the grease Mary, she told me. Then she pointed at another crack in the concrete with another water stain 30 feet away, "but so is that one."

What distinguishes this Mary is that it is a Guadalupe Mary, she said. The Virgin appears cloaked in the garments of an indigent, she said, and that sounded totally plausible to me since I identify the Fullerton exit with homeless men holding signs begging for food.

What sealed the deal for her were the rosary beads formed by a line of crystallized salt that, as she said, proved God works in mysterious ways.

Watching the TV news crews arrive and set up their microwave feeds reminded me of my time as a cub reporter for the *Chicago Sun-Times* when I was assigned to report on the last days of The Dying Poet of Romania. The year was 1972 and the four major newspapers in Chicago were engaged in what may have been the last big city circulation war in America.

I worked for Field Enterprises, which owned the morning *Sun-Times* and the afternoon *Chicago Daily News*. The competition was The Tribune Company, which had the morning *Tribune* and afternoon *Chicago Today*.

In those days, the distinction between a morning and afternoon newspaper was already blurred. The *Sun-Times* published an early Bulldog edition aimed at hitting subway platforms by 5 PM for the evening rush hour home; not to be outdone, the *Daily News* and *Chicago Today* put out a Green Streak edition every morning at 9 AM to trump the morning papers with their version of the day's events.

Thirty years later, the competitive instinct has been passed along to the broadcast and cable news outlets with their 24/7 schedule; and I'm sure it's only a matter of time before ordinary citizens are sending off news of miracles like the Virgin under the Viaduct using instant pictures snapped on their cell phones.

But I was talking about The Dying Poet of Romania. That story began — as did this one — on a slow news day when the *Daily News* published a story saying a dying poet from Romania would be flying into O'Hare in the afternoon for a special medical procedure that would save his life.

When he stepped off the plane, literally dozens of photographers, TV crews and newspaper reporters mobbed the arrival gate. None of them expected the others to be there, so they followed his wheelchair down through the terminal thinking the others would fall away. But the gaggle of reporters only grew larger. Once out on the street, while the news cameras were setting up for a press conference, the reporter for *Chicago Today* pulled up in a rented limousine to take the dying poet to the hospital in comfort.

The poet was whisked into the backseat, and *Chicago Today* was on the streets a few hours later with a full report— and what the editors called his "Dying Poem."

Not to be outdone, a *Tribune* reporter later than night managed to sneak into his hospital room and obtain a second dying poem. By the time I got to work, the *Daily News* had yet another dying poem — and my editor at the *Sun-Times* was pissed.

I was sent over to the hospital with instructions not to come back without a dying poem; and that is where I spent most of the day monitoring the poet's condition, which was remarkably stable. When I called in on deadline, the editor wanted to know if I had a dying poem. "I've got dozens of them," I said, "the guy has written books of them. We just need a translator."

In the lightning speed of the newspaper wars, my efforts were quickly turned into so much birdcage liner. For the dying poet to receive the required medical procedure, it turned out he needed political asylum. So the vigil outside his hospital room was soon supplanted by stories of public-spirited politicians working on the asylum problem.

For the next week or so, every newspaper, every day, had some tidbit about the dying poet. He sat up and drank liquids today. He met with his family. He urged his many fans to pursue world peace. He got neither better nor worse. Mainly, he just got more legal. By the time the Immigration and Naturalization Service got around to issuing the order saying he could stay, he had disappeared off the front page and was living with his daughter in Oak Lawn and resting up from the surgery.

For a story like the Virgin Under the Viaduct to work in today's media, we all have to suspend our journalistic disbelief. Antonio Mora, the Channel 2 anchor, must be willing to tease a story about "what some are calling a miracle." Ron Magers must with a straight face ask whether it's a water stain on the wall of a viaduct or is it the Virgin Mary? And observers like Wilson Vasquez must state the obvious. "It all comes down to faith. If you have faith, you will see it."

By the end of the week, things were starting to die down under the viaduct (thanks in no small part to a cold snap). That's when CNN showed up and NBC's Today Show stepped in to take the story national.

And that's not all bad, says Ricky Brown, 37, who's been sitting against a light pole on Fullerton for the last few days holding a sign that says "HELP I'M HUNGRY." Before the crowds started coming, Brown liked to work the exit ramp near the stoplight for spare change. That spot is now occupied by satellite trucks.

After a hard winter, Brown says he was so desperate he fell on his knees last Sunday and prayed to God for a sign his life wasn't over. It came the next morning in the form of a TV news truck. And for the moment, at least, his life on the street isn't all that bad. In fact, the pickins are pretty good.

— April 22, 2005

Never Leave Your Block

Poolside at the Park

I spent the afternoon Tuesday poolside at Holstein Park, and not alone. My view from the water's edge is a sea of bobbing heads and writhing torsos. Twenty minutes after it opens, the Olympic size pool is filled to its 300-person capacity. With the temperature hovering in the low 90s, a hundred more swimmers stand in line outside waiting for someone to leave.

To sit by a public pool in Chicago is to watch the unbridled enthusiasm of youth. The mostly teenage kids couple and de-couple in mock water fights, ride piggyback on each other, venture forth into the deep end and, just as quickly, retreat back to the shallow. Some wear goggles, others tattoos. There is a contingent of young women who have staked out a corner of the deep end deck — that which holds the sun longest — for reading, tanning and talking on their cell phones. Four boys do flips off the side of the pool nearby, should any of the girls care to notice.

A wide-angle scan of the scene reveals such a remarkable tableau of diversity in that pool that you can't help but believe you are in Barack Obama's post-racial America. Who is black, brown or white hardly matters; there are so many shades of each so closely packed together they are like brush strokes on a Degas painting. One notices more who is fat, thin or just plain scrawny; whose swimsuits barely cling to their hipbones; and whose belly falls wantonly over the top.

There are 18 strollers lined up next to the kiddie pool. Although the pool never gets deeper than a foot, half the children bask in its glory and half cling to the edge until mom, dad or nanny lead them in.

The lifeguards are a trip unto themselves: temporary help, mostly college students on summer vacation, probably ushered into the job by helpful parents who know the park district's obtuse hiring rules. My favorite, Simon, who sports pink spiked hair, is off today. But the others dutifully sit on their observation towers, life preserver in hand, watching the clock until once an hour, on the hour, they blow a whistle, empty the pool, and see whether there are any bodies left under the surface.

What I like about Holstein Park, and all the parks in Chicago, is the very public nature of them all. While the pool overflows with swimmers, summer camp kids play baseball on one diamond and kickball on another. All the kiddie swings in the playground are filled. Blankets are spread out under shade trees. Mothers sit atop them, a toy chest full of trucks, plush dolls and balls scattered around them as if they've brought their living room to the park for a day.

Across the street is Senior Citizens Park, a small grove of trees with a sidewalk winding through. Four winos sit on a bench drinking beer out of bottles in paper sacks. A homeless woman pauses to rest with her plastic satchel of belongings on a ledge decorated by tiles children made at the last Bucktown Arts Fest.

There is commerce in this park, none of it authorized by the park district. A bicycle cart vendor named Morelia sets up outside the playground to sell ice cream bars. She announces her arrival with a fanfare of "La Cucaracha" car horns. Two seven-year-old neighbors sell lemonade from a folding table under their mom's watchful eye.

It's summer in Chicago. A time to let the cares and woes of winter go. (Not that they will disappear.) Yes, it would be great to get away, but there are plenty of options if you can't. Holstein is one of 552 parks in the Chicago park district. They contain 33 beaches, 51 outdoor pools, 16 lagoons and 10 bird and wildlife gardens.

If you haven't been to the lakefront lately, take the bus down and see what's new. (Don't drive. Trust me, the parking lots will be full.) Play volleyball at North Beach. Sit out under palm trees at Oak Street. Try the beach at Promontory Point in Hyde Park or, if you have a dog, doggie beach at Montrose Harbor.

If you're looking for simple peace and quiet, check out the secret lily pond in Lincoln Park or the Art Institute gardens downtown; or pick a tree, any tree in any park, and lie under it reading a book.

It's summer in Chicago.

— June 24, 2009

Harry is Moving Out

I can see him out my front window every day now, sitting on his front stoop surrounded by house fans, yard tools and other knick-knacks he's accumulated over the decades he's lived in the neighborhood.

Harry is moving out. Not to Florida or Arizona like those other snowbirds following their retirement plan. Harry Kugelman doesn't retire. He just moves on. He's found a new place up on Cicero Avenue — a condo where there's no stairs to climb because, at 78, Harry has climbed his share of stairs — but he can't take all his stuff with him. So he's offering it up to his neighbors at a good but fair price in a yard sale.

Before Harry decided to turn his front stoop into a Dollar Store, he was the watchdog (and unofficial historian) of our block. He knew who was coming and going. In all too many cases, he knew the apartments they were moving into or moving out of, and the people who had lived or died in them before.

He'd been there that night with old man Kowalski when his son got married and Kowalski expired half from joy, half from exhaustion. He'd seen that house at the end of the block turn over three times, once to a drug dealer, and it never was the same after. He could tell you who was sick, who was unemployed, who fought with his wife and who had found redemption in the local church group.

Harry has been keeping track of Bucktown's affairs since he was born here in 1926 a few blocks away on Leavitt. But as much as the neighborhood has changed, what happens with the people in it doesn't.

That is not to say Harry was here for everything. He enlisted in World War II and missed a spell from 1944 to 1946, but he's been a pretty regular observer since he got back, and he hasn't missed much.

He remembers The Depression in the 30s. "Those were hard times. We had funeral parlors all over the place, every corner, and you could go to a wake a week if you wanted," he recalled. "No money and disease going around like the plague. Lot of people don't remember, but I do."

After the World War II, Harry came back to try his hand at running a grocery store, driving a delivery truck and doing a little of this and that until 1967 when he was hired by the city health department. He bought the red brick bungalow across the street for $6,500 at auction. It was his life's savings at the time — and a rounding error in the price the new owners are paying for it.

In his almost 40 years on our block, Harry never married. But he had lots of friends. He made them one at a time walking around the neighborhood buying groceries, going to the hardware store and sitting on his front stoop saying "Hi, how's it going?"

Harry's yard sale has attracted a lot of attention in the neighborhood. My wife has purchased three pink ceramic teacups, several mixing bowls and a rust-removal brush to clear old paint off our iron fence. As a bonus, Harry threw in six cans of black spray paint. ("You can only buy it now in the suburbs because of the gangs," he said. "So I got extra.")

Bill, the cop down the street, bought Harry's old ladder and step stool — just to keep him from using them — and has made Harry a solemn promise that he will remove the waterbed Harry's tenant left before he changes the light bulb above it for the new owner. If he hadn't, Harry was vowing to do it himself.

Harry is not selling his belongings as much as he is placing them in a good home. He has a rope clothesline — "That's not easy to find." — that the woman down the street could use; and some old silverware that isn't much, but might work for the young couple who just moved in. Stop by Harry's stoop and you'll hear him say, frequently, "It'd be a shame to just throw this out."

Harry's new condo is supposed to be quite fine. Air-conditioning, carpeted floors and a kitchen with a microwave oven and automatic dishwasher. "It doesn't get fancier than that," Harry said.

From Harry's first days in the neighborhood to his last, he's watched the swirl of ethnic change from German to Polish to Puerto Rican to gentrification. "It's just the people that change, not the problems. So I talk to them and if there's a problem, I say why don't you try this," Harry said. "I'm just here to help when I can and listen when I can't."

I'm going to miss you, Harry. We never talked as much as we should have. But it's been a comfort seeing you out on the stoop keeping watch over the neighborhood.

A man's home is his castle. And from watching you sell off all your belongings I've learned a hard lesson. What we accumulate as treasures in our life is valuable only to our friends as mementos. So make as many friends as you can — and invite them to your yard sale — because there's a lot of stuff to get rid of.

Goodbye, Harry. Your teacups and spray paint are in good hands. And I'll be re-painting that iron fence any day now.

— June 25, 2004

The Holstein Park
Adult Basketball League:
A 7-Part Series

A Season for All Reasons

(This is the first of a 7-part series following the exploits of the eight teams in the Holstein Park adult basketball league.)

At night, when I walk the streets of Bucktown, I can hear the distinctive squeak of sneakers and dribbled basketballs coming out of a second story window of the Holstein Park field house telling me there is a basketball game in progress.

The field house is a landmark, a hulking edifice built in 1912 to bring more recreational opportunities to the working classes on Chicago's west side. The sound I am hearing 93 years later comes every Tuesday and Thursday night from an adult basketball league that still plays in the Holstein Park gym.

There are eight teams in the league. Each represents some facet of Bucktown's racially mixed population and, it turns out, every division within it. On any given night, you can find 18-year-olds playing 50-year-olds, gang-bangers playing yuppies, college grads playing high school dropouts — men of all ages, races, incomes and backgrounds mixing it up on a basketball court, where none of that matters.

For the last few months, I have been going to the field house to watch the games and, every week, I learn something new about the teams, the players and their reasons for playing.

They play under names chosen by the teams — Lito's Weapon, The POWs, Dipset, Papa's Moustache, West Haven, Latin Express, Fullers Brew Crew and The Old Fockers. As you might suspect, there is a story behind every name.

The rules of the Holstein Park Adult Basketball League are not like those in other leagues. By current standards, the Holstein gym is a cracker box so players must make some accommodation. A professional basketball court these days is 94 feet long by 50 feet wide. This one is 45 by 36. And that's a wall-to-wall measurement with six inches between the out-of-bounds line and the gymnasium's brick walls.

Because of the small size, teams can only put four players on the court at a time. Players who are not playing sit in an 8-foot wide bench area at one end of the court. Spectators can watch the action from a similar postage stamp-sized cage above it. If either players on the bench or spectators above want to see whether a shot has gone into the basket, they have to lean out into the court and look up — or down — at a backboard that is bolted to the overhead gallery mesh.

When the Holstein Park gym was built, basketball was still a game played with baskets. Nets with the bottoms cut out were not introduced until 1917. After every score, play was stopped for a new jump ball at center court. Under those rules, the room was plenty large enough.

But that was an era when basketball was a game of set shots and two-handed passes. In a new era of crossover dribbles, no-look passes and double-dog-dare-you reverse dunks, the Holstein gym can easily make teams feel like they are playing inside a pinball machine.

When you walk into the Holstein Park gym for the first time, you are reminded of what it must have been like in the days of yore. The brick walls have been varnished so many times they are stained brown. There's a warm, oily wood smell to the air. The ceiling is held up by wood beams, and sky-lights are the chief source of illumination. If you close your eyes, it's not hard to imagine rows of men in white leggings and moustaches doing calisthenics or tossing medicine balls to and fro.

At the start of every game, Adrian Loza, the recreation director, gets out a metal rod and cranks open the upper windows for ventilation. There is no air-conditioning. It's not comfort but competition that draws teams to the Holstein Park Adult Basketball League. When I first started going to the games, the season was already five games old. The Old Fockers were playing against Papa's Moustache, but neither team was tearing up the court.

During the warm-ups, Papa's Moustache looked to be the stronger team because it was filled with young college grads. Teddy Harris, 24, said the team was mainly a bunch of his friends who recently graduated from Marquette University in Milwaukee and found themselves working in Chicago and living within a few miles of each other in Bucktown. Joining the league was a way to carry on their friendship, stay in shape and talk about their jobs without just sitting around in bars.

In the beginning, everyone was enthusiastic. Choosing a name might have been the high point of their season. After many beers, they decided to call themselves Papa's Moustache after a racehorse in the 1970s known for coming from behind. They would be the Papa's Moustache of the league, the team nobody noticed until the end — when it couldn't be stopped.

The entrance fee was easy enough to raise, and the team agreed the T-shirts shouldn't be the cheap kind, but 100% cotton with cool graphics. Unfortunately, making their way as young professionals in Chicago soon took the players in different directions, and their enthusiasm for playing basketball was one of the first bonds to break.

By the fifth game, as good as the team was, Teddy began to realize he was lucky to be able to field the minimum three players required before a forfeit. Even with a full team, it was a rare night the come-from-behind Papa's Moustache had enough reserves on the bench to actually come from behind.

The Old Fockers are Papa's Moustache ten years later. Ten years further along in their careers, with wives and children in the picture, they joke about fighting off senility the way Sammy Sosa jokes about taking steroids. The realities of life require a little self-deprecating humor, and so they call themselves The Old Fockers.

The team is the brainchild of Mike Bernstein, 40, a freight cartage broker, who owns a three-flat across from the park. Bernstein is short and prematurely graying, with a middle-age paunch around his belly; but he's a more than passable ball-handler who exudes competitiveness and, in practice at least, has a deadly shot from the corner.

For the 15 years Bernstein has lived across the street from the park, he's watched Bucktown gentrify from his living room window. He's seen the drug dealing through the fences around the basketball court and the gang-bangers staking out their benches in the park. But he's also seen the slow change in the games on Holstein's outdoor court as artists and college students and young professionals, emboldened by their growing numbers, started using it.

A few years ago, Bernstein and his wife had their first child and, looking for inexpensive day care nearby, discovered the tots program at Holstein Park. It was during one of those parent observation nights, while Bernstein and the other dads in the program were watching their 3-year-olds show off their tumbling skills, that the dads came to realize the time had come when they too ought to be exercising.

Bernstein suggested they join the Holstein Park adult basketball league. He found takers in Steve Lipe, 38, a real estate developer; Trey Rasmussen, 35, an executive with BP/Amoco; Paul Stepan, 35, a commercial real estate lender; Rob Sciachetano, 34, an insurance underwriter; and Mike Hartnett, 34, a sales manager for a plastics company.

Because they needed a little talent to go along with their enthusiasm, Bernstein recruited Mark Roswig, 36, a former tenant, and Joe Backer, 25, another freight broker at his firm. Both had actually played college ball even if, as Backer admits, he was only on the junior varsity at St. Joseph's in Michigan, a small Division III school.

It did not take long for The Old Fockers to become marked men in the league. In the second game of the season, a rag-tag team of gym rats playing under the name of Dipset beat them by 67 points — in a 40-minute game. The game instantaneously became legend, and other teams who played The Old Fockers felt winning by any smaller margin was a defeat.

On this night, Trey Rasmussen was out on the court shooting free throws when Bernstein walked into the gym talking on his cell phone. "Yeah, but he said he'll be here, right?" Bernstein said. "Okay, say goodnight to her for me. Love you. Be home soon."

"The hardest part is being sure we'll have four guys," Rasmussen said. "We spend all day exchanging emails on who's coming, but you never know who's going to show up. And if you can't get more than four, you have to play the whole game without substitutions."

At the last minute, Stepan and Backer show up. The game between The Old Fockers and Papa's Moustache begins. It is a low scoring affair. Neither team is especially interested in ramping up the pace because neither has any reserves.

Somewhere around the middle of the second half, I wander upstairs to the gallery. There is only one other spectator. One of the players waiting for the next game is a man wearing a bright jersey that says POW. He calmly monitors the action (or lack of it).

I take a seat next to him. Just as I do, Teddy Harris from Papa's Moustache explodes to the basket with a two-step leap over two startled Old Fockers.

"I don't think these Old Fockers can hold up," I say. "They'll fold, you watch."

"Yeah, kids these days, they're all run and gun," he says. "They'll wear you down pretty quick. But maybe The Old Fockers will surprise you."

He introduces himself as James Howard, one of the player/coaches on the POWs. Howard admits he himself is 50 — 12 years older than the oldest of The Old Fockers — and Howard doesn't even care if he gets to play. He just enjoys coming to the gym to watch the action. So we go back to watching, but now I am curious why he plays on a team called The POWs.

"You don't recognize me, do you?" he smiles. I look at him again but draw a complete blank.

"I'm your mailman. We call ourselves The POWs because we are your Post Office Workers. Get it?"

James and I watch The Old Fockers and Papa's Moustache duke it out right down to the last minute. With 40 seconds left to play, the score is 54 – 49. The Old Fockers are ahead by 6 points.

The referee whistles a foul, and two free throws later Papa's Moustache narrows the gap to 54 – 51. They steal the ball and score again. It's now a one point game, but the Old Fockers are still ahead 57 – 56. With nine seconds to play, they can taste their first victory.

After a hard day at the office, fighting traffic on the Kennedy to make the game, changing with no time for warm-ups, saying goodnight to their 3-year-olds on a cell phone, and forced to play 40 minutes with no substitutes, they are nine seconds away from victory.

But not tonight. Papa's Moustache steals the inbound pass and Harris drives the length of the court to hit a deuce at the buzzer.

The game ends Papa's Moustache 58, Old Fockers 57.

— May 6, 2005

The Gym Rats

I went over to Holstein Park again tonight, arriving just in time to see The Old Fockers get shellacked by the brew crew from Fuller's Tap. The winning margin was 23 points.

The gym rats were cackling.

"Don't get discouraged," Shelton shouted. "You beat the spread."

"What do you mean?" asked Trey Rasmussen, one of the mainstays on The Old Fockers.

"The ref had you — and 25 points," Shelton said.

In every park, and every high school, and every place in America where basketball is played, there are always some kids who seem to live and breathe gymnasium air. They cannot walk without dribbling a basketball between their legs, pass a hoop without throwing something at it, or see a game without stopping to critique it. Like other gym rats, Holstein Park's contingent starts gathering at the park as soon as school lets out and hangs around on league nights until the last buzzer sounds.

The first to arrive are Shelton and Cyrus Moore, 15 and 17, two brothers who have been coming to the park since they were in grade school. Shelton is a freshman at Roberto Clemente High School and a starter on the freshman basketball team. He is stick thin and only 5'4", but makes up for his lack of height with playful bravado and a sharp tongue.

His older brother Cyrus, 17, is more reserved, but a wizard when it comes to dribbling basketballs off stairs, water coolers, walls and the backs of unsuspecting friends. When Cyrus is happy, he is very happy. A grin the size of a pizza slice spreads across his face. But when he not happy, he falls into a dark and brooding silence.

After the Moore brothers arrive, Dante "DT" Fitts, 16, a starter on the Senn High School team usually shows up. Then, always late, comes Rob Da'Jon Duren, 16, a sophomore at Lincoln Park High School. They call him "Mutombo" because every ounce of muscle in his 6' 2" body has been pulled into long taffy string arms and legs that resemble Dikembe Mutombo, the 7'2" back-up center for the Houston Rockets.

Most of the gym rats play together on a park team in the afternoon high school league, but the action, they all know, is in the adult league at night. So they cling to their patron, Tony Lopez, 20, who used to be one of them, but now works at O'Hare airport transporting coffins in the cargo terminals.

Too old to play as a park teenager, Lopez last winter decided to put up the fee for the adult league and fill his roster with his gym rat friends. Besides Mutombo and DT, he recruited Vic DeJesus, 22, and Vic Hubbard, 20, whom they call "Black Vic" from a church league down the street. But his best catch was Rufus Lacy, 26, a former star on the powerhouse Westinghouse High School team, who used to work with Lopez's brother in the warehouse at Best Buy.

Tony lives and breathes basketball. (Wouldn't you if your day job was transporting dead bodies?) Although he's only 5'6" himself, he's the perfect point guard, always looking for ways to pull more players into the mix. To build team spirit, he let the team choose their name, and they voted to call themselves Dipset after a rap group from Harlem whose song "Crunk Music" was the flavor of the month at the time. "Who cares what you are called? What matters is winning," Tony told me. For Tony, it's all about winning.

For Lacy, it's a different story. In some respects, he doesn't actually want to be at the gym. He's not lazy, he tells me, and he's not dumb. He works hard, and his goal in life is a steady job he can build into a career. It just hasn't happened yet. After Christmas, Best Buy scaled back the warehouse jobs and he was laid off. His confidence needed a little boost so Rufus turned to the one thing he knows best.

On the court, he's a natural, always in control, always in the right place at the right time. In the Dipset offense, the 6' 4" Lacy is the lynchpin in the lane. "Tony is always trying to get me on his team," Lacy explained to me one night. " I didn't want to play this year because I need to look for a new job, but he's hard to turn down...and basketball is something I'm good at."

Although Dipset is not playing tonight, the gym rats congregate at the park anyway to watch what they anticipate will be a preview of the championship game. Lito's Weapon, now leading the league with a 7-0 record, will be playing West Haven, second in its division at 5-2.

Lito's Weapon is the sentimental favorite of the park staff and, after their own team, most of the gym rats. If you can imagine the gym rats at Holstein Park ten years ago, you would have its entire line-up. Brian Kelleher, 28, and Alan Erickson, 30, Rob Mihalski, 25, and Antonio Velez, 24, all come from blue collar families in Bucktown and, even though one or two still plan on going to college, they all still work and live within a couple of miles of the park. Kelleher is a logistics supervisor up the street at the Target store. Erickson is an electrician. Mihalski, whom they call "Country," works construction; and Velez, or "Q", is an assistant coach at Kelvyn High School, where he played on the varsity as a teenager.

Rounding out the team are Danny Garcia, 24, and Moses Seda, 20, who were young enough to be mascots to the gang back in the old days, but are now full-fledged members of the team. No matter what kinds of things they might have fought over ten years ago, this gang of Irish, Polish, Swedish and Puerto Rican kids has come through it all together as a team.

"It's fun playing with these guys," Kelleher says. "You don't have to worry about stupid stuff like how we'll get along. We all know so much about each other. We know who everyone is, and what they're going to do."

What inspires the team this year is the missing seventh man, Lito Velez, 20, everyone's favorite friend and a former teammate. Last November, on a street corner just a block south of the park, Velez was shot dead in a drive-by gang shooting.

So they are playing this year as "Lito's Weapon" and have dedicated their season to finding Lito's killer.

While Lito's Weapon warms up at one end of the court, the West Haven team gathers at the other.

Eugene Woods, the 46-year-old coach, takes off his street clothes at courtside. When he lifts his shirt, the jersey reveals that West Haven is sponsored by State Sen. Rickey Hendon on behalf of a "Better Life for Youth" — a program for troubled teens that Woods has run for almost two decades in the Henry Horner housing projects.

One look at the West Haven players shows that youth is a flexible concept. Besides Woods, the West Haven roster includes Greg Turner, 32, a clerk in a downtown law firm; Ty Kirby, 30, a former King High School star who works at a hair products warehouse in Blue Island; Randy Mason, 23, a fork life operator in the O'Hare cargo area; Corey Evans, 30, a neighborhood activist; Alonzo Pruitt, 31, whose occupation is somewhat undefined, and two other players, Martell Thompson, 28, and Daryll Lane, 32, also known as "Bone," whom you might call ringers.

Woods has assembled his West Haven team this year as he has in the past from the playgrounds on Chicago's west side. It is territory he knows well. He grew up in the projects just north of the United Center and attended Crane High School where he played varsity on the baseball, basketball and football teams. In 1979, he went to Kansas State on a baseball scholarship, but soon discovered Kansas isn't Chicago and returned to Chicago to work in the community.

Woods is what is known on the west side as a playground scout. He's one of those shadowy figures you find standing outside the chain link fences in the parks watching kids play ball. Occasionally, if he spots a genuine diamond in the rough, he might call a coaching friend at St. Joseph's, or Simeon, or another basketball powerhouse where the kid might get noticed enough to be offered a college scholarship.

But Woods doesn't stop there. He keeps tracking the talent long after they're out of high school. He knows who dropped out, who's back in the gangs, who's selling drugs, who went to jail, and who's getting out. He knows when his players are fighting with their girlfriends, or need a job or just want a friend. By always having a team going, he always has a way of connecting. "I know most of the really good players on the West Side," he boasts, "but you have to get them when they are available."

This is the first year a Woods team has played under the West Haven banner. The name is a concession to the Chicago Housing Authority attempt to re-brand the old projects as a new "mixed-income" community they are calling West Haven.

As many as 1400 apartments in the old Henry Horner high rises have been torn down in the last few years, replaced so far by 450 new low rise apartments in developments next door. But much of the poverty and most of the problems remain. The medium income of the neighborhood remains around $10,895 and 38 percent of the families live below the poverty line. Kids in the local elementary schools read in the 27th–35th percentile of Chicago students. Only 70 percent ever get to high school. And only 40 percent of those in high school ever graduate.

One of the most nagging problems, though, is adult unemployment, which hovers around 50 percent. With no jobs to be had, players can always find a pick-up game on the playground courts. This gives Woods a wealth of talent to choose from, but it can also be a drawback. "I had a really great 3-point shooter and ball-handler last year," he told me. "But he went and robbed a bank so we were at a real disadvantage during the playoffs."

The West Haven players are slow to arrive so while we wait, I introduce myself to the referee, Matthew Mohammed.

Like most of the refs who work Chicago Park District games in the neighborhood gyms, Mohammed, 45, is a high school coach picking up a little spending money on the side. For the last six years, he's been the varsity basketball coach at Collins High in Chicago. He started his coaching career as an assistant to the late Willie Little at UIC then coached other college teams in Elmhurst and at Malcolm X.

Before he became Matthew Mohammed, the ref, he was Matthew Pepper, a star himself at Creiger High School who played in the glory years of the late 70s against the likes of Mark Aguirre and Skip Dillard at Westinghouse, Terry Cummings at Carver, and Russell Cross at Manley. He once put up 26 points against Aguirre in the city semi-finals, but nobody was scouting him. So when Aguirre went on to DePaul, Mohammed accepted a scholarship to Chicago State — where he played, coached and graduated, as many of his teammates did not.

Mohammed is sharing with me his stories of his coaching days with Willie Little, himself a Chicago high school legend, when "Bone" arrives — just in time to save West Haven from a forfeit.

Bone is wearing baggy blue jeans, a leather Pelle-Pelle jacket, and a "buck-fifty baseball cap" (so named because custom versions are sold on West Madison for $150). The cap's lid is a silky laminate snakeskin that Bone has had stitched in rhinestones on all four sides with the names Malcolm X, Lil Buck, Big Dog and Lil D.

Before he undresses, I ask Bone what the names on the cap represent. "They're friends of mine who died," he says.

Adrian Loza, the Holstein recreation director, notes that we are running late so Mohammed blows the opening whistle and the two teams go at it, driving up and down the court — not that it takes many steps — exchanging baskets at a furious pace.

It's a strong, physical game. Kelleher and Erickson are big forwards in the Luc Longley mold who patrol the paint like it's their own private property. The only player on the West Haven team who can match up is Martell Thompson, who, at 6'8" calls himself "The Determinator" because, when he steps into the game, he changes the outcome, he says.

Martell is determined to play that role here. He steps to the top of the key then charges to the basket like Michael Jordan on a tear. The ref blows the whistle to call a charging foul.

"What kind of fucked up dumb call is that?" Corey Evans shouts from the sidelines. Woods, standing beside him, glances up in the air, but says nothing. Corey paces up and down then flips the ref the bird. "Get eyes, man, get eyes!"

Mohammed stops play and calls a technical foul.

A few minutes later, Martell makes the same cut to the basket. This time he is draped in the arms of the defenders, but the ref holds back on the whistle. "Hey, you faggot ass ref, get a clue!" Corey shouts.

Mohammed again blows his whistles and signals another technical foul.

"You're blind, ref, you're blind." Corey won't let up. He paces and tosses a towel onto the floor. Since he is the only authority on the court, Mohammed calls yet another technical foul and ejects Corey from the gymnasium.

But Corey won't leave. He storms onto the court screaming, "I'm going to kick your motherfucking ass!" Woods and Bone finally grab him and walk him to the door. Adrian dials the cops on his cell phone.

It takes all of two minutes for the police arrive. Two policemen walk in, followed by two more, and two more, and two more. Before you can say 'what happened?' there are ten officers inside the field house, and four squad cars parked outside. But Corey is long gone.

"What can I tell you," Adrian says later. "These cops like me. Nobody's going to let anything bad happen in my park."

The first half ends with Lito's Weapon up 34–30, largely on the strength of the three technical fouls against Corey. Woods makes a point of reminding his team that, but for the technical fouls, West Haven would be ahead. Neither team is ready to throw in the towel so the second half starts off just as intensely as the first.

With five minutes remaining, and the score knotted up even, West Haven calls a time out.

"We've got to keep them off the boards," Kelleher tells his teammates in the huddle. "Box 'em out. Crash the boards. Play the D. Play the D." They double clap and run back onto the court.

"We're not in bad shape. We got better athletes than them," Woods tells his team. But West Haven is dragging. The players take their places back on court. Just then, Woods sees Ty Kirby poke his head through the gym door.

Kirby looks like he has just woken up. He didn't think his West Haven team was playing until the second game, so he doesn't actually have his jersey. Woods strips off his and hands it over. By the time Kirby has changed, there are only three minutes left to play. Nonetheless, Woods calls a special timeout so Kirby can check himself in at the scorer's table.

When play resumes, Kirby, standing off to the side, seems out of place. The inbound pass finds its way into his hands and he pops it up for a 3-pointer. On the next play, the ball is tapped over to him again, and he drops another 3-pointer.

In the span of the next 90 seconds, he adds another 3-pointer, two jump shots and, on a foul, a free throw — 15 points in three minutes.

The game ends: West Haven 79, Lito's Weapon 67.

"Who is that guy?" I ask Bone.

"He's pretty good, isn't he?" he says.

"He's great!" I say.

"Yeah, when he shows up," Bone says.

— May 13, 2005

A Grudge Match

By early March, match play in the Holstein Park Adult Basketball League has settled into a steady rhythm. The games are not spectacular, but each is its own little culture clash. Tonight, the boys of Dipset are paired up against a Puerto Rican team called Latin Express from the other side of Western Avenue, and West Haven is back to face off against the Post Office Workers.

When I arrive at the field house, the gym rats are hanging in the lobby. Mutombo leans back on the stairs crushing program flyers in one hand and launching them off as jumpers toward an open garbage can. Tony Lopez races around making sure all his team is going to show up. The Moore brothers, Shelton and Cyrus, are still talking about the "incident" the other night when the cops were called.

"I heard he had a gun," Shelton says. "They were afraid he was going to hang out afterward and shoot somebody."

Adrian, the recreation director, walks through carrying the scoreboard panel up to the gym.

"Hey, Adrian, he had a gun, didn't he?"

"No, he didn't have a gun," Adrian sighs. He hates the way these kids blow things out of proportion. "But if something like that happens, it never hurts to have cops around."

As game time approaches, the gym rats move up the stairs to the gym. When they turn the corner, Tony sees Rufus Lacy, the last unaccounted for man on his team, changing out of his street clothes.

"Where were you, man? I thought we'd have to play without you," Tony says.

"My car got towed," he says.

Shelton breaks into a hysterical giggle.

"Don't laugh, man! It costs me a lot of money to get out. You want to pay me back?"

Shelton falls silent. Tony sees that Rufus is out of sorts, so he rallies the others on the team. "Come on, none of that matters," he says.

The Latin Express team has been on the court warming up for almost 15 minutes. Their coach is Juan Salinas, 34, a sheriff's deputy who discovered the league when he was driving by the park a few years ago and saw a banner on the fence.

Salinas, his friend David Cruz, 31, and two brothers, Javier, 36, and David Crespo, 34, all grew up together around Palmer Square. In the summer, they play together on a softball team in the Humboldt Park league. For the winter basketball season, they've added Javier's son Jonathan, 18, a senior at Kelyvn High School, and Alvaro Diaz, 25, who works for Javier at the Dominick's on California and Belmont.

Bucktown can be a little like a Balkan state. Over the years, it's been a port of entry for immigrants from Germany, Poland, Russia, Puerto Rico and Mexico. Even as the real estate developers lure in young professionals with new condos and McMansions, there are always pockets of neighbors who refuse to let their blocks get re-developed for the next new thing. The block where Salinas and the Crespo brothers grew up is one of those. Everyone on Latin Express proudly lives and works within a few miles of where they grew up. The seasons change, the sports change, but the team remains the same. And every year, Salinas tells his team the same thing: this is our year.

Once Adrian has the scoreboard plugged in, Mohammed, the referee, calls the players from Dipset and Latin Express to center court for the opening jump. When they are all in place, he looks around and laughs.

"Okay, everyone with jewelry take it off!" he says.

The Dipset players walk back to the sidelines and begin dropping bracelets, rings, earrings, pins and nose clips on the scorer's table. The booty falls on the Formica in a rhythmic clang. The players on the Latin Express more discreetly put their jewelry back into their duffle bags. Back at center court again, Mohammed blows the whistle and the contest begins.

There's not much to say about the game. Latin Express is practiced, organized and well-condition. But only the youngest of them, Jonathan Crespo, has the street ball savvy to keep up with Dipset's playground moves.

For most of the game, Latin Express stays within striking distance. But as the clock winds down, Jonathan's outside shot deserts him just as Tony Lopez finds his range. Tony drops in three 3-point shots and the score is suddenly 79–67 with only a minute left.

On the sideline, Mutombo has been swinging his arms around and telling anyone within hearing distance, "I can feel my windmill coming on."

Everyone on the team knows what he means; so, with time running out, Tony calls a timeout and brings Mutombo in for Rufus. He spreads his team to the corners, opening the lane for Mutombo to sweep in on an alley-oop pass and "windmill" the ball into the hoop. There isn't a person in the gym who doesn't know what's coming.

But once in the game, Mutombo seems to forget the clock is ticking. He just stands out in the corner warming up his arm, oblivious to the seconds dwindling away.

Tony jams the ball under his arm and shouts at him. "Run to the hole, dumb ass." Suddenly, Mutombo looks at the clock and breaks for the basket. Tony lofts the alley-oop. Mutombo grabs it with both hands and slams it down — only to see the ball carom off the rim at the buzzer.

The second game pits the POWs against West Haven. Eugene Woods, the West Haven coach, still smarting from the ejection of Corey Evans, tries to convince me his team is better off without the distraction.

"Corey's going through a lot of personal stuff, so I had to suspend him from the team," Woods says. "But we're trying to win the championship here. We won it two years ago, and I really like the guys we have this time, so we have to stay focused."

Woods is breathing easier these days because his ringers, Martell and Bone, are both on board for the playoffs. In the early going, Martell had to miss some games because he was in Juice The Loose's tournament over in Rockwell Gardens. A CTA bus driver and basketball fanatic, Juice is famous for staging a basketball tournament in the housing projects that soaks up all the good playground on the west side. Now that the tournament is over,

Martell and Bone mix easily with the other West Haven players, who are goofing under the basket until game time.

Across the way, my postman James Howard introduces me to the rest of his POW team: Wilbert Parker, 46, his co-coach; Eric Patton, 26; Maurice Pleasant, 34; Jesse Reed, 29; and Ontario Hopson, 24. All work as mail carriers in the Logan Square station on California Ave.

This is the team's fourth year in the league, Howard says. Although it's been suggested they could win it all with only a little outside help, there are no ringers in the bunch. The postal carriers believe that if they play by the rules, they will win by the rules. But it doesn't hurt that Hopson is a 6' 8" recent transferee who played college ball at Olive-Harvey College.

The POW warm-ups look like they came right out of the civil service manual. Before every game, the team arrives early. They walk in clockwise fashion around the perimeter shooting jump shots. After each has taken five shots, they run lay-ups, then each takes five free throws. The routine never varies, and no one breaks the routine.

Although both teams are made up entirely of African-Americans, they could not be more different. One thrives on organization, passing and waiting for the good shots. The other freestyles from one playground move to the next, somehow making ends meet. The result is a culture clash as severe as any in the league — and more than a little animosity brews just under the surface.

In tonight's game, freestyling wins out. West Haven jumps out to an early lead and sets a rapid-fire pace. The attack comes alternately up the middle on drives by Martell or from the edges with 3-pointers from Ty Kirby, Bone and the suddenly hot "Z" Pruitt. By halftime, the score is West Haven, 54, POWs 27, and there's no reason to think the postal workers can catch up.

Only minutes into the second half, Ty and Martell start showboating. Martell grabs a long lob under the bucket and, in a single step, he is up, over and dunking the ball. The Ref blows the whistle for a foul. There's no dunking allowed in this league.

A few minutes later, in an almost identical play, Martell takes another long pass and drives to the basket again. Again, he rises up over the hoop then gently waits while he falls back to earth. Just before his feet hit the floor, he finger rolls the ball over the lip of the hoop for another basket. Martell drifts back on defense with a sly grin across his face. The ref too smiles.

Mohammed has seen it too many times before. If only this kid...he thinks to himself...hadn't dropped out of Crane High School, he'd have been varsity for sure. He probably would have been offered a college scholarship. He might have had a shot at the NBA. Even without the NBA, he could be a coach, a lawyer, a team leader. Now he's a 28-year-old unemployed playground player; and the only people who will see this talent are in this tiny Holstein Park gym, the place where all the might-have-beens come to be.

When the buzzer sounds, the final score is West Haven 122, POWs 64. The good news for the postal workers is that their overall record, 7-3, is good enough to get them into the playoffs next week. The bad news is their first opponent will be West Haven.

"Hey Adrian," Woods shouts, "Can't we just take this game, spot them 50 points, and call it over?"

"It's the playoffs," Adrian replies. "Anything can happen."

— May 13, 2005

Lito's Weapon

Moses Seda, 20, the young spark plug on Lito's Weapon, was alone in the Holstein Park gym cleaning up for the adult league games when I found him.

In my first couple weeks at the field house, I'd taken Moses to be another of the gym rats. As we spoke more, I learned I was wrong. Moses works mornings as an auto parts clerk at Pep Boys, afternoons as a recreation director at the park, and when he's not playing basketball, he can be found in church at night rehearsing for a play or home practicing with his rap group "Wodey Click".

The basketball, the church play and the rap group are all things he would have been doing this year with his cousin Lito — except Lito is dead, shot multiple times in the chest last November in what police describe as a "gang-related" incident.

So when Moses talks about his rap group, he says he is dedicating its next album to FUBU (which was Lito's rap name); and when he talks about his team, Lito's Weapon, he notes that everyone on the team has dedicated this season to Lito because he and everyone else on the team — Alan, Brian, Country and Q — know "Lito wasn't no gangbanger. You check around," Moses says, "Lito was straight. Everyone liked Lito."

According to the police report, that may have been the problem. In the long and involved story of gangs and Holstein Park, the gangs have been on the losing end of a 10-year gentrification process for some time now, but Moses knows it hasn't always been that way.

Shortly after he was born, Moses' father was killed in a gang shooting and he was left with a grandmother who raised him up to avoid the gangs.

"She won't have any part of it," he says. "But you know how it is. You grow up here, you know who's doing what. You may not be in a gang, but you know who the gangbangers are. They're the kids you grew up and went to school with. You can't avoid them."

Ten years ago, the Latin Kings and Spanish Lords fought a turf war for control of Bucktown that is recounted in a book titled *My Bloody Life: The Making of a Latin King* by Reymundo Sanchez (a pseudonym). Although all the names have been changed, many of the neighborhood kids claim to know someone in the book and can provide a block-by-block accounting of which gangs still hang out in which local parks.

In the last few years, gang activity has been pushed further south and west of Holstein Park. An influx of wealthy young white professionals, an active community group and new neighborhood policing techniques (like the alderman's decision to take down the outdoor basketball hoops near a drug-dealing corner) have reduced gang-related shootings by more than 50 percent this year. So the shooting of Anthony "Lito" Velez, 20, stands out, if only because it's one of only a handful in the last year.

Velez had been a standout baseball player at Amundsen High School. After graduating last June, he was enrolled to begin college in January. He had no criminal record. "He was one of the good guys," one policeman said. But that wasn't necessarily the case with the friends he hung out with, one of whom has a long record of juvenile gang-related arrests.

According to the police report, at 8:50 PM on the night of November 17, Velez and his three friends were walking to their car on Dickens Street when a black Lexus SUV approached them. The occupants rolled down a rear window and words were exchanged. The friends fled. Lito did not. Shots were fired. Lito sustained multiple gunshot wounds to the chest. By the time police got him to St. Elizabeth's hospital at 9:25 PM, he was pronounced dead. Four unknown male Hispanics in dark clothing were being sought.

A few days after the shooting, there was a funeral service for Lito at God's Army Church on Kedzie and Chicago. Moses was right, everyone in the neighborhood knew Lito. Almost 600 people turned out.

But no one came forward with any new information on the shooting. One of the neighbors said the vehicle might have been a green GM Jimmy. Another heard an engine backfire, but couldn't say where it came from. Of

Lito's three companions on the night of the shooting, one suddenly felt the need to go to Arizona; another said he was inside with his mother; the third said he ran before the shots.

"You know how the gangs get jealous of the guys who can get out?" Moses speculates. "That was Lito. He was on his way to college. He'd made it. These gangs around here didn't like that so — you know how it is — it's 15–16 year olds doing what other people tell them to do. Somebody said kill Lito. So they did."

It would be another couple days before I could get back to the park to see Lito's Weapon play Papa's Moustache. In the meantime, I'd gone over to the Shakespeare Avenue police district and spoke with the detective investigating the murder.

Lt. Mark Hawkins, the head of detectives for Area 5, said police have sifted through a number of leads, but they've reached a point where they need help from the community to solve the shooting. Because Velez had so many friends, they believe there's talk about the crime in the community that they are not hearing.

"It's the same as 90 percent of the murders we see," Hawkins said. "We know who the victims are and, in most cases, we know who the shooters are. What we need is a witness. Someone who'll step forward and say 'I saw it.'"

In the gym, the game is delayed while Teddy Harris of Papa's Moustache tries to round up enough of a team not to forfeit. At the scorer's table, Moses is clowning with some of the gym rats. He's pumped because earlier in the day a New York record company named Desert Storm asked for a copy of his rap group's CD.

Moses has decided, with all the questions I'm asking, I must be writing a book. When it is published, he wants to make sure I've got the details on the rap group (which is sure to be well known by then) so he takes pains to explain the name of the group and his label. "We're on the FUBU Ill State Records label," he says. "FUBU, because that's my cousin, and Ill, because that's like Illinois, but on the street it means raw, you know, like bad."

"And we call the group Wodey Click because"— Moses notices me writing furiously in my notebook— "Wodey, that's W-O-D-E-Y. You know, like when someone says 'What's up homey?' Wodey's the same thing. 'What's up Wodey?' Wodey is like homey, so we're a Wodey click."

I ask him if that's spelled C-L-I-Q-U-E. He hadn't thought of it that way, but Moses likes it. "That's rad, maybe we can change it," he says. "Our group is going to New York next month to play it for Desert Storm. They're like phat in rap, so then we want to take it to California, and all around."

I tell Moses that I stopped by police headquarters. He doesn't immediately respond. I pass along Lt. Hawkins' request for more cooperation and tell Moses, as Hawkins told me, the police think there's talk about the crime in the neighborhood they're not hearing.

"There's more to it than that," Moses says slowly. "Our family, we know Lito was no gangbanger. But we're going to find who did it. You hear me? We're going to find who did it. "

"And we still honor Lito's memory," he adds. "Every Sunday, we go out to the cemetery to stand at the graveside. Last week, there were maybe 40 of us, mostly family, but his friends too, you know. Somebody will maybe say some words about Lito...or there's a prayer...and we'll all hold hands. It's our way of saying we won't forget."

When Teddy's efforts to turn up a third player for Papa's Moustache fails, Adrian, the park recreation director, spies Cyrus hanging nearby and suggests he be given a special exemption to play. For Cyrus this is like being asked to join the Bulls for the night because Michael Jordan has the flu.

Even with Cyrus on the court, Lito's Weapon has four players on the floor against Papa's Moustache's three and jumps out to a lopsided lead. But with all his friends watching, Cyrus could not be happier running up and down the court with the big men. By game's end, he personally has put up 41 points in a 124–95 loss.

For Cyrus, this is a whole season in a single game. And in that game, maybe a whole season in a single play. It comes late in the second half when Cyrus, only 5'4", drives recklessly into the lane between the two 6'4" defenders.

He uses every move he's got to slip between them — the crossover dribble, the behind the back spin and, finally, his under the basket reverse lay-up. It circles the rim twice and falls in.

As he runs back on defense, Cyrus is beaming ear-to-ear with that pizza slice grin. It is a joy to behold. *The joy of basketball.*

— May 27, 2005

The Old Fockers Go Down

I took my camera over to the park last night to take one last round of team pictures before the playoffs. The evening promised a rematch between The Old Fockers and Dipset, the team that famously beat them by 67 points. With only two games left in the regular season, the opportunities for The Old Fockers to redeem themselves are running out.

When I walked into the field house, something was awry. Mutombo was standing in the lobby on crutches and Shelton was dribbling a basketball around him, taunting him for his clumsiness. In a pick up game at school, Mutombo apparently came down hard under the basket and fractured his ankle. The doctor said he will be out for three weeks.

Tony Lopez, 20, the coffin wrangler at O'Hare and team captain, was not particularly worried. He still had Rufus...and the opponent, after all, was just The Old Fockers.

Plus, the gym rats had more important things to worry about. Cyrus had just gotten a new cell phone — a Psychic II from T-Mobile — and he was still figuring out all the buttons.

"It's got everything," he said. "Camera, cell phone, text messaging, games. I can do AOL instant messenger and Yahoo Messenger." He flashed it around in front of his friends, but few were impressed. Each one pulled out his phone and began to compare features.

"What's your ring tone?" someone asked.

"I'm still working on that," he said.

"You need games? I got games," Mutombo offered.

"You ain't got game, nigger," Shelton said, "You got a bum foot."

"I'll take you," Mutombo says, rising up on his crutches and chasing Shelton out onto the court. "Come on, you and me, one on one."

Once Mutombo is out on the court, he can't help but take a few shots. He drops his crutches, hops to the free throw line and tosses it up. The doctor's orders are less than two hours old, and already Mutombo has broken them.

All day, The Old Fockers have been trading emails trying to get a team together. But it's still not clear who will show up. Mike Bernstein, the coach, won't be there because he's got Bulls tickets. Mike Hartnett, the plastics salesman, has fallen off the radar. Trey, Joe and Rob keep warming up waiting for one more man. At the last minute, Steve Lipe, the developer, shows up.

"Good news," I tell Trey, "you've got your fourth."

"Now we have to play," he sighs.

The game starts on a high note for The Old Fockers. Trey hits a three and they have the lead — for all of 2 minutes and 15 seconds. The boys from Dipset are disorganized and lackadaisical. They hot dog up and down the court, tossing up trick shots and hopeless long bombs. The four Fockers, meanwhile, play a measured, steady game. At halftime, they are only down 5 points: 37 to 32.

When the second half starts, the Fockers hit two quick baskets to pull into a tie, then hang even with the Dipset up to the final minutes. Eventually, they have to call a timeout to catch their breath. Tony's slashing attack at the basket and Rufus's dexterity are taking their toll. Dipset goes up 70–60, then stretches it to 80–71 and finally 90–71. But the Old Fockers could not be prouder. They'd cut their losing margin from 67 to 19.

"I think that's the best game we've played so far," Trey says. "It feels a lot better than those games where you lose by a couple points when you should have won," said Steve.

Off the court, Cyrus has gone back to peering at his new cell phone. He wanders around the gym with his eyes glued to the screen.

"Have you found your ring tone yet?" I ask.

"Yeah. Here, listen. I'm going with 'Neva Eva' by Trillville."

He pushes up the volume and plays it for me.

Mutombo walks by and leans in to listen.

"That's bad, man. That's good bad, you know what I mean?" he says.

Two days later, The Old Fockers (0–9) are back for one final game against Latin Express (3–6). With a victory tonight, Latin Express can capture the last spot available in the playoffs.

The regulars — Mike, Joe, Paul, Rob, Mark and Steve — have all come to participate in this last game. Only Trey, who has made every other game, somehow has a conflict. Everybody on The Old Fockers feels like they have a pretty good shot, but no one wants to say it aloud for fear of jinxing it.

Over the last two months, The Fockers have gone from a loose affiliation of dads looking for a little exercise to a team that naturally organizes itself on the court, each player falling into a role the others understand.

So confident are they of their newfound familiarity, they now try a few no-look passes during games and — occasionally — catch them. Everyone knows where Steve will set up in the paint, when Mike will take his corner jumper, and how Joe likes to post up just off to the side of the key.

Playing together, with two reserves to spell them, they hang within a half dozen points of Latin Express until, with only 1:26 remaining in the game, Joe Backer comes up with a hot hand. He hits two 3-point shots from the outside then he is fouled in the act of shooting. He drops two free throws to cut the margin to one point.

The Fockers call a timeout, more to rest than map strategy. Twice before they've been this close — and blown it. This time, they have a plan. It's pretty simple. "Let Joe shoot." He's the one with the hot hand.

When The Old Fockers return to the floor, Jonathan Crespo, the lightning quick 18-year-old Latin Express guard, steals the ball and the Fockers' strategy is out the window. They are forced to foul, then hope for a missed free throw and a rebound.

And so the game ends in a series of fouls and free throws — not with a bang but a whimper.

After the final buzzer, both teams walk instinctively to center court like they are in junior high school again. They line up opposite one another and the players walk toward each other, shaking hands, offering their congratulations for a season well played.

The Old Fockers, the smartest team in the league, have finished their season 0 – 10, the worst record in the history of Holstein Park Adult Basketball League.

— June 3, 2005

The Playoffs

Jesse Reed walked into the Holstein Park field house alone and went immediately to the pop machine. He plunked in a dollar for a diet soda. No time
for dinner tonight. It's playoff time.

This is the fourth year Reed, 29, has come to the playoffs with his team,
the POWs, and he has no plans to go home disappointed. "We've got to win,
we just have to win," he says. He has plenty of reasons for optimism. It's not
just that the new uniforms have arrived — finally. This year they also have
the talent, one Ontario Hopson, a 6'8" center who, only a few years ago,
anchored his Olive Harvey college team.

On the day Hopson walked into the Logan Square post office on
California Avenue, Jesse remembers saying to himself, "We have to get this
guy on the team. If he's on board, this is our year."

Tonight, the POWs first game in the playoffs is against West Haven.
Over the course of the regular season, the POWs and West Haven have met
twice and come away with a split decision. Unfortunately, the last part of the
split was a 122–64 pasting the POWs took just before the playoffs began.

All weekend, Reed had been stewing about how to reverse the outcome.
He wants to be a leader this time, to get to the gym early, but not so early
as to appear over-anxious. He walks up the stairways to the gym only to
discover he is the last to arrive. All eight other POWs are already out practicing. Reed changes quickly and makes it onto the court just in time for the
opening tip-off.

West Haven is playing tonight without the benefit of their coach, Eugene
Woods. He is taking his young charges in Sen. Hendon's youth program
on a Spring vacation tour of southern colleges. But Woods' regulars are all

there —Ty Kirby, Randy Mason, Bone, Greg Turner and Alonzo "Z" Pruitt—everyone but "The Determinator" Martell Thompson, who shows up about midway through the first half.

For the first few minutes, it looks like the POWs have the upper hand. Hopson controls the lane but passes it out so his teammates can take their outside shots. When Martell shows up, the momentum shifts. He locks horns with Hopson. Now free from rebounding duties, Bone and Ty Kirby tie up the less athletic postal workers on defense and, on offense, pour in three pointers. By halftime, the score is West Haven 41, POWs 29.

The lopsided scoring breeds dissention in the POWs huddle. Hopson complains there are too many big men on West Haven that the other POWs aren't covering. He can't play both offense and defense on the boards, he says. Howard urges the team to stay calm and pass more. Reed insists that when he's open no one gets him the ball.

The second half begins much as the first one ended. Their lead has made West Haven all that much more confident and, without Woods there to enforce teamwork, they are freestyling like it's playground time after dark. The older POWs can't keep up. But Reed isn't going to let this game slip away so easily.

With only four minutes left — and West Haven ahead by 20 — Reed calls a timeout from the sidelines and checks himself into the game to replace Jesse Howard. The ref is confused. Suddenly, there are five POWs on the floor. The referee asks them all to sort it out. To make peace, Howard sits and lets Reed play. But nothing changes. The blowout ends West Haven, 79, POWs 47.

The season is over for the postal workers. Everything except the recriminations and second-guessing that are sure to follow. Both teams go to the bench to change, but Jesse can't let go.

"You guys got nothing," Reed shouts across the gym at West Haven. "You got nothing!"

"Oh yeah," Bone shouts back. "We got a team."

"We got a team," Jesse responds.

"You got a losing team," Bone says.

For Latin Express, making the playoffs is another occasion for a family party. They arrive for their game against Dipset with a cheering section of wives, kids, cousins and girlfriends. Juan Salinas, 34, the coach, scurries around making sure everyone has a comfortable place to watch. His excitement is contagious.

But the boys on Dipset are also pumped. Tony, Rufus, Dante, Vic and Black Vic are running a disciplined lay-up line while Mutombo, showing no signs of his ankle injury, stands under the basket handling rebounds.

Both teams appear evenly matched in size and talents — neither has a towering player in the center — so after 20 minutes Latin Express goes into halftime with a one point lead.

Tony is not happy with his team's performance. Rufus has kept them in the game with tough rebounding and defense in the lane, but their outside shooting stinks, especially Tony's. In the first half, Tony has thrown up 11 attempts and made only 3. And Mutumbo has been all but useless.

Instead of mapping strategy with his team, Mutombo spends his halftime complaining to the referee about alleged fouls that weren't called. Matthew Mohammed, the referee, listens patiently at the scorer's table, but all he can do is smile. When Mutombo finally walks away, Mohammed laughs.

"He's just young," he says, "When he gets some meat on those bones, he won't feel every touch. Mutumbo thinks a stiff wind is a foul."

Tony's frustration at his poor first half shooting only makes him re-double his efforts in the second. His first two long shots drift wide of his mark and Rufus, hoping to calm him down, shouts, "You don't have to do it all alone. Look for the cutters."

As soon as Tony eases up, the kids on Dipset step up. Dante comes into the game and hits two quick jumpers, one for three points. Then Mutombo, who's been staying wide of the hoop for much of the game, mixes it up under the basket for a crucial rebound and a put-back bucket. Suddenly, Dipset is up 67 to 51. Their swagger is back.

Latin Express calls a timeout to regroup; the boys from Dipset, at each other's throats only minutes ago, are hanging on each other's shoulders, exchanging high fives, confident they can't be caught.

The Latin Express pulls back to within nine points, but they're reduced to a series of desperate fouls at the end. With only ten seconds left, Mutombo grabs a rebound and stands holding the ball until the clock runs out. But Jonathan Crespo, 18, won't go down easy. The smallest player on the court wraps his arms around the tallest for one last, deliberate foul.

"Finally, Mutumbo gets his foul," Dante says. But he misses the free throw. The game ends Dipset 75, Latin Express 66. Dipset has won a place in the championship game.

Beating the postal workers did not put West Haven into the championship. It only moved them along to a bigger challenge: Lito's Weapon, the neighborhood favorite.

Lito's Weapon had a 9–1 record and decimated most of its opponents in the division. It rode on the shoulders of its two big men, Brian Kelleher and Alan Erickson, but Rob Mihalski— the 25-year-old they call "Country"— Lito's cousin Antonio, or "Q", and Danny Garcia were strong outside shooters. And then there was Moses Seda, the heart and soul of the team, guarding its legend of Lito as carefully as any man on the court.

When I enter Holstein Park for the final playoff game, there is only one person in the gym. He is Ty Kirby, the outside shooter for West Haven who'd startled me the first time I saw him by draining 15 points in three minutes — even though he showed up only five minutes before the end of the game.

Somehow, Kirby had gotten the start time of the game wrong — again.

He'd driven up all the way up from his job warehousing hair care products in Blue Island, fighting traffic on the Dan Ryan for two hours, only to discover he was an hour early.

When I approach him, Kirby tells me this is his first year on Wood's West Haven team. He joined as a favor to his dad, who plays with Woods on his softball team in the summer.

"Mostly, I just like freestyling, but in this league, I get to do a little tournament and a little freestyling. It's good to mix it up."

I ask where Ty played in high school. He says he started out at Orr High School, then in 1990, Landon Cox recruited him for the King High School team that won the city championship and went on to the state championship finals in Springfield.

"Were you a starter," I ask.

"I was in the beginning," he says, "but coach benched me because he said I wouldn't play defense, and he was right. But I am kind of famous."

"Oh yeah?"

"Yeah, I was in that movie *Hoop Dreams*."

"You weren't William Gates or Arthur Agee, I know that."

"No, but you know that scene where Marshall was playing King. I was in the crip line [doing lay-ups] when they had a good close-up of me. I wish I had a dollar for every time they showed that."

At the opening tip-off, Moses is paired against Martell, who is not only six inches taller, but 50 pounds heavier. He tips it to Q who throws up a long shot that falls wide. And they are off.

For the next twenty minutes, both sides go at a frantic pace, up and down the court with picks, no-look passes and in-your-face lay-ups. This is one of those games where the small gym plays like a pinball machine. Players from other teams, waiting for the second game, crowd into the little bench area to watch.

For twenty minutes, it is a glorious game of basketball. There is no one hero on either side, and no specific turning point. Everyone plays well. Everyone is a hero. But gradually the tide turns to West Haven. By the middle of the second half, Country's outside shot has gone cold. Q has no problem dribbling between defenders up the court, but there's no one open to pass to. Kelleher and Erickson pick up hard fouls under the board.

When Martell drives the lane to take the West Haven lead to 18 points, Moses calls a time out. He leaps up and slams the wall, then stalks around the court cursing only himself. There's not enough time for Lito's Weapon to stage a comeback, a fact Martell makes sure everyone on his team understands.

"They have to catch us," he says. "Take your time. Play out the clock. They have to catch us."

And that is just what West Haven does, slowing the tempo and drawing more fouls from a team that has few to give. When the game is out of reach, Woods pulls Martell out to play the last couple minutes himself.

Martell takes a seat on the bench, spreads out his legs and begins singing. "Sha Na Na Na...Sha Na Na Na...Hey, hey, goodbye."

But he isn't much into the thrill of victory. He's thinking about the tournament prize money, now only a game away. "How much is it?" he starts asking around on the bench. "How much do we get if we win?"

After supplies and ref fees are paid, it's traditional for the Holstein Park recreational staff to split the remaining team fees into 1st, 2nd and 3rd prize money. First place is worth about $475. There's $250 for the second place team about $100 for the team that wins the consolation game.

Coach Woods has promised his team that he will split the winnings with them if West Haven wins. As he steps off the court, Martell is already thinking about the money. "One more game, right? How much do we get if we win?"

No one on Lito's Weapon wants to talk after the game. I ask Kelleher what happened.

"We played lousy," he says. Not much in the way of sports quotes, but pretty accurate.

At the gym door, I see that Bone has changed into another of his sartorial outfits, this time featuring a loose blue silk shirt, baggy white pants and another buck-fifty cap. This one has "Chicago Cubs" sequined across the front and carries tributes to Terrance, George and RIP Duke.

"How many of those caps do you have?" I ask.

"I got a lot of them," Bone answers. "I got a lot of dead friends."

The Championship match will be West Haven vs. Dipset. For all the marbles — and $475.

— June 10, 2005

The Champs

By the time the Holstein Park Adult Basketball League gets around to playing its championship game, many of the players are on to their next season. The finals were supposed to be in late March, but a flurry of interest in the NCAA tournament (based on the appearance in the Final Four of The University of Illinois) pushed it back by unanimous consent into the first week of April.

A season that began with the sound of dribbled basketballs in winter's darkness is ending to the crack of bats on balls in the lengthening sunsets of spring. Ten below had become sixty above. Another winter has passed. The park maintenance staff is cleaning the Holstein pool for a Memorial Day opening. Summer is just around the corner, and there is still no champ in the Holstein Park league.

The consolation game in the upstairs gym between Lito's Weapon and Latin Express proves to be as unimportant as its name. There are no spectators.

Even Moses Seda, so passionate only two weeks before in his desire to win one for Lito, skips the game to attend a play rehearsal at his church. His absence leaves Lito's Weapon with the minimum three players, who then lose to the Latin Express in a contest that is not even close.

With t-ball, softball and soccer teams practicing in all corners of the park, you have to be a dedicated fan to snake out the league finals that evening in Holstein's upstairs gymnasium. But Tony Lopez is one dedicated basketball fan.

It is still two hours away from game time, but Tony is patrolling the parking lot like a hawk, circling the ball fields waiting to pounce on his Dipset team. Black Vic arrives first. Then Vic DeJesus and Mutombo show up. Finally, Rufus appears. All players have a game face when they get serious. But Rufus has something more, a Ninja warrior headband pulled low above his eyes. He offers a quick hand bump hello to his teammates then goes directly upstairs to warm up.

While Tony waits for his last teammate Dante ("DT"), one of the outer ring of gym rats, a 15-year-old named Dennis, starts parading around in his new Nike Air Jordans. Tony can't help but laugh.

"Hey, I heard some shorty got killed for those shoes," Tony says. The morning paper that day had a story of about a teenager shot by someone who wanted to steal these same Jordan gym shoes. "Took 'em right off his feet and sold them for $30. Can you believe that?"

"These are $250 shoes," Dennis says defensively.

"Not on your feet," Black Vic chimes in.

As game time approaches, Dipset heads up to the gym to warm up. Everyone except Tony who scours the playground one more time for DT, his 16-year-old reserve forward. He finds him making out with a girl behind the baseball diamond and, like an irate parent, hauls him off upstairs to the gym.

"Where'd he come from?" Vic asks.

"Tony found him standing out on the Fullerton exit with a sign saying 'will play for food'," Black Vic jokes.

"Come on, man, I'm just chillin'. I'll be ready." Dante says.

West Haven has shown up for its championship game without Coach Woods. The last game of the season has also run into the critical final weeks of the legislative session in Springfield. As much as Eugene Woods loves his basketball, he loves his Better Life for Youth Program more so he is there, needed or not, to fight for every state dollar he can get.

Even without Woods, most of the team has shown up ready to play — everyone except Martell Thompson, "The Determinator." Ty Kirby came up in the afternoon from the hair products warehouse in Blue Island. Randy Mason, the forklift driver at O'Hare, and Greg Turner, the law firm clerk downtown, left work early to beat the traffic. Bone and Alonzo Pruitt, not tied to particular work hours, were waiting for them under the basket running what some teams call a warm-up drill.

Without the 6'8" Martell, there's no clear choice who will play the center post for West Haven. "Don't worry, Martell is always late," Bone says. And, indeed, the game starts with Bone and Rufus facing off at center court because Martell is nowhere to be found.

From the opening jump, it's a run and gun game. Trey Rasmussen, one of The Old Fockers, joins me on the sidelines to watch. He nods appreciatively at every off-balance shot and playground move he sees. "This pace would have killed us," he says.

At this rate, both teams are well on their way to scoring more than 100 points. The problem for Dipset is that — at halftime — they have thrown everything they've got at West Haven, and West Haven still holds a 57–45 edge. "It's a case of the men versus the boys," Rasmussen muses.

"These guys all know how to play street ball," he says. "That's how they beat us. But the West Haven guys have been around longer. They can shift into a control game and Dipset doesn't know how to deal with that. It's one thing to go out there and trade three-pointers in a run-and-gun game. But you can't do that when you're down 12 points and, suddenly, the other team is playing ball control. It's all strategy then," he says. "The kids just haven't been around enough to make that transition."

As the second half begins, Rasmussen's words prove prophetic. Rufus and Black Vic, who've played on solid high school teams, set picks for each other and dish out backdoor passes. But Mutombo ignores them and keeps launching outside jumpers like they're spitballs. Tony is so frustrated and anxious to make up the deficit he dribbles up court and shoots as often as he gets the ball. When Tony is hot, Dipset is hot. But when Tony is not, Dipset is not.

West Haven extends its lead to 85–54, then 95–66 going into the final two minutes. This game is over. Tony takes himself out to let Dante play the last minutes. It's garbage time. Ty throws up a full court prayer shot from one end of the court to the other. Even a frustrated Rufus finally drops his center post discipline to power in a lay-up down the lane (just to remind them he can).

With the score 103–73 and ten seconds on the clock, Mutombo doesn't want to be left out. He cranks his arms around a couple times in his famous "windmill" and drives to the basket for one final over-the-top dunk. The game ends on a whistle. A technical foul. There's no dunking allowed in the Holstein Park Adult Basketball League.

In the weeks following the end of the season, I discovered seasons don't end, they transform into the next season. But you can't spend this amount of time with a story without wondering what happens to the people after it's over. So this is what I can report:

Despite their 0–10 record, Trey Rasmussen told me The Old Fockers are proud of their performance. "We have street cred now," he said. "I was walking past the park with my wife and kid the other day and we ran into Cyrus. He acted a little embarrassed, but he smiled and gave me a high-five. My wife didn't know what that was about. But I felt really cool."

At Pepe's Groceria on Saturday Mutombo told me he'd just come from a tryout in Washington Park for a TV reality show called "Batttleground." With sponsorship from Nike, the producers are flying six teams of playground players this summer from Chicago, New York, LA and other inner cities to compete at the famous Rucker Park in Harlem for a show that will air in the fall on MTV.

Mutombo is one of 15 players chosen for Team Chicago (and one of only two 16-year-olds). He leaves on July 8 for a six-week, all expenses paid vacation in New York this summer. Sweet.

Tony Lopez still works at O'Hare airport transporting coffins and is organizing a new team of gym rats for the fall basketball season.

Eugene Woods, the coach of West Haven, has entered his softball team in the Holstein Park summer league and is among the current division leaders. His Better Life for Youth program is considered one of the great successes in Chicago Human Services and has been renewed for funding.

But Lito Velez is still dead and the Chicago Police Department reports his murder remains an active investigation.

— June 17, 2005

The Politics of Neighborhood

A Tree Grows on Burling Street

A Chicago TV station recently ran a little snippet in the evening news about a developer in the 1900 block of North Burling who was temporarily blocked by local residents from cutting down a 100-year-old silver maple tree in front of his new mega-mansion

Anybody but me would have chuckled at the report and moved on. But I remember that tree because, when I came to Chicago, my first apartment was across the street.

Burling today is Chicago's new Astor Street. "Gazillionaires' Row," the *Chicago Tribune* calls it, a place where Chicago's wealthiest families are tearing down 2-flats to build $20 million and $30 million homes — and now, a $40 million French Revival mansion that will span seven lots, according to the TV report.

Settled by German and Hungarian immigrants at the turn of the century, Burling Street never amounted to much beyond another link in the middle class grid of Chicago neighborhoods. Hard working Europeans in the 1920s gave way to hard working Puerto Ricans and African-Americans in the 1950s. Then, in the 1960s, they too started to move on, pushed out by a younger crowd of young white professionals looking for cheap rents near the hip nightspots of Lincoln Park.

When I arrived in August 1972, it was a moonless night and all the streetlights were out. I had driven down from Milwaukee to take a new job as a reporter for the *Chicago Sun-Times*. All my worldly possessions were packed in the back of my little red Toyota. There was an eerie silence as I carried my boxes upstairs to my new apartment. The only signs of life were little eyes peering out from behind curtains watching me move in.

I didn't know what to make of my new neighbors until I woke up the next day to read the lead story in the *Sun-Times:* "Girl Shot on Street of Fear," the headline screamed followed by an account of a drug deal gone bad — you guessed it — just across the street from my new apartment.

I do not know if there was any better job in America in the early 70s than being a reporter in Chicago, nor did I care. Chicago was then in the throes of its last great newspaper war. Four major dailies — *The Sun-Times, The Tribune, The Daily News* and *Chicago Today* — turned out round-the-clock editions aimed at cannibalizing each other's readership. Local TV stations were expanding their 6 o'clock news briefs from 15 minutes into full-fledged newscasts (using a new technology called video) and an earnest group of English majors from the University of Chicago was starting to publish a free weekly called *The Reader.*

I was 22 years old, the newest recruit in editor Jim Hoge's attempt to give the *Sun-Times* a fresh look at a fast-changing city. He had already promoted a young University of Illinois grad named Roger Ebert to be its movie critic and turned a ne'er-do-well newspaper journeyman named Tom Fitzpatrick into a columnist who won a Pulitzer Prize for his 1969 account of the SDS Weatherman "Days of Rage."

He brought me down from the *Milwaukee Sentinel* and, over a bowl of fresh strawberries and cream at the Tavern Club, offered me $12,000 a year to come work for his paper. This was a 50 percent bump in my salary, so I accepted on the spot. (And that was the last time I saw the inside of The Tavern Club.) My deskmates in the *Sun-Times* newsroom that first year were Bob Greene, Eleanor Randolph, Roger Simon, Andy Shaw, Mike Flannery and Paul Galloway (perhaps the best writer of us all).

Every morning, Greene would conduct — with his typical aplomb — "Love Hour." This was his way of reminding me about my pitiful attempts to find a girlfriend in a new city. He was constantly offering to set me up with the perfect girl — the most memorable being a 6' 6" Amazon who ran a pregnant women's clothing store — then grilling me on my scores.

Every night after the last deadline passed, I would join my colleagues on an excursion into the Bermuda Triangle of journalism — Riccardo's, O'Rourke's and the Old Town Ale House — so named because they were tavern hangouts with cascading closing hours. Many great journalists were lost there; and, occasionally, a few were found.

As impressed as I was with my colleagues, the most memorable character I met that year was my downstairs neighbor, Sarah Nance, a divorced nurse with three children who looked like Catherine Deneuve and acted like Simone de Beauvoir.

Sarah lived her life without a dime to her name. But she lived it to the fullest. She was a bohemian at heart, having grown up in a Czech family on the southwest side. She was beautiful, smart and funny — not a bad combination — with a flair for adventure that no one could resist.

She was most at home in the kitchen. She could make out of nothing in the refrigerator a meal everyone heartily enjoyed. Her sister Mary Terese lived across the street and was a frequent guest. So too was a heroin-challenged drug user on the block named Capp (for his astrological sign Capricorn) who often volunteered to babysit her children — and sometimes showed up. On more than one occasion, her boyfriends (including Ebert, for a while) would join us for long, intoxicating Sunday dinners that stretched well into the night.

It's hard to look at Burling Street today and see much of what it was like back then. Halsted Street, only a block west, was then considered the western edge of civilized Chicago. Most of the storefronts were boarded up, except for Gepperth's Meat Market, a butcher shop from the old days, and Manhandlers, a meat market of an entirely different kind for Chicago's secret gay community. Those same store signs now read Barneys, Benetton, Cynthia Rowley, and Ralph Lauren.

At the end of our block, there was a vast wasteland of broken glass and dirt clumps we called "The Prairie." This misguided city venture into urban renewal has since turned into a landscaped Oz Park; and the rundown Waller High School on its southern edge, which attracted a steady stream of students from Cabrini-Green past our house, is now an International Baccalaureate program with selective enrollment.

Not a day went by on Burling that I wasn't reminded I was living in exciting, but dangerous times. I remember one afternoon when Sarah's kids — ages 6, 8 and 11 — found a gun in the alley behind the house. The cops showed up and went door-to-door looking for the owner. Sarah called me at work.

"Can you maybe get them to stop? They're scaring my kids," she said. Before I could explain my job did not include halting police investigations, she blurted out, "I put it in the garbage can. I only got it because my ex was getting out of jail. Somebody must have gone through our garbage. Isn't that an invasion of privacy?"

There was always some piece of Sarah I would never know, but that only made life on Burling Street all the more exciting.

On my first Thanksgiving in Chicago, we put on a feast worthy of Ben Hecht and Harriet Monroe in their heyday.

Ebert bought the turkey. Hank DeZutter brought over a cooked goose he'd prepared himself. Anyone who arrived early was given a task in the kitchen, and anyone who arrived late crowded into her little living room. Hank Oettinger, the inveterate letter-writer who agnostically filled all the editorial pages in all the papers, settled into the only easy chair. Sydney Harris, the kindly photographer and veteran of the Spanish Civil War, played on the floor with Sarah's kids.

At one point, it seemed like O'Rourke's closed and its patrons had been poured out into Sarah's living room. Jay the bartender was there. So were Jim and Micaela Tuohy, Karen Conner, Paul McGrath, John McHugh, Ed McCahill, Nancy Day and G. Bob Hillman. So many now famous names it's hard to include them all.

Sarah was in her element, flitting about offering up her famous "ants on a stick" — celery with raisins and peanut butter in the grooves. She would serve and gossip and laugh and move on. When it was all over, she turned to me. "That was a pretty good party, wasn't it?" she asked. Like she had just thrown a party, but not attended it.

Nothing good ever lasts. In 1974, Sarah fell in love with the barbell magnate next door. I followed a bad instinct and moved further west with them to an even more dangerous neighborhood called Wicker Park. We pooled our money to buy a former rooming house under the el tracks on Caton Street and moved in. Sarah and her three kids, Bob and his four English mastiffs, and me. But that's another story.

When they take down that tree on Burling — as I'm sure they will — the memory of those days will be 34 rings in from the outer bark. It's not like that tree was watching me come of age in Chicago. It was just the sentinel on watch at the time looking out for us in reckless times.

But the new homeowners on Burling Street will have something else to worry about. What happens to the spirit of the girl shot on the street of fear once it is unleashed from its wooden tomb?

— December 1, 2006

Winter Tow Zone

One of the dirty little secrets of Chicago's winter parking ban is that I started it. Not alone. But I was there in the summer of 1979 when Jane Byrne strode into the mayor's office after Michael Bilandic's lapse in snow removal and, under pressure to do better, called together her city department heads and her new media consultant, *moi,* to prepare for the upcoming winter.

The Mayor had set aside $40 million for the task, and her new head of Streets and Sanitation was proposing a new winter parking ban on 107 miles of city streets. From December 1 to April 1, every night between 3 and 7 AM, city tow trucks would clear all major thoroughfares; and if the snowfall exceeded 2", they would tow cars along 500 more miles of secondary streets.

My job as the media consultant was to sell this plan to the public, which I did by creating a cute little Skippy The Snowball who marched in the Christmas parade, graced the cover of brochures, and appeared on TV in helpful public service announcements urging citizens to heed the warning signs — or kiss your car goodbye.

I was reminded of my little friend Skippy when, 21 years later, I stood in the city car pound at Grand and Sacramento waiting to retrieve my own auto, an early victim of this year's winter parking ban.

The weather was a balmy 37. A light drizzle — but no snow — had left the ground soft and muddy.

Outside the locked chain link gates, protected by concrete traffic barriers meant to prevent irate citizens from crashing into the payment trailer, an enterprising canteen truck driver was doing landslide business serving coffee to people pulling up in taxis.

Inside the trailer, a line of 40 motorists snaked through a ragged rope line waiting — for what turned out to be two hours — to present evidence of ownership and $150 cash or credit card to retrieve their vehicle.

The citizens were not in the best of moods. Behind me, a man from Wisconsin was making his second pass through the line with a copy of the car title his wife had just faxed to his hotel. Ahead of him, two brothers clutched notary public papers transferring car ownership between them since one had a valid driver's license, but the other appeared to be the actual vehicle owner. Another woman leaned sleepily against a wall waiting to shuffle forward a few steps when the line moved.

Retrieving one's vehicle from a city car pound, it turns out, puts you in touch with one of the most inept systems of government in the world.

The workers, as a rule, are the meanest, dumbest and slowest in city government, which says a lot. Their workday friends and colleagues are private tow truck drivers, an occupation favored by certain people who, because of certain questions regarding their criminal background, are often doing this only "part time." And their clients are mostly out of sorts, often hangover, angry people with whom they communicate through a series of makeshift signs, in Spanish and English, taped to the wood paneled walls warning of various dire consequences if one were to act rowdy, assault an employee or, worst of all, enter the yard without a permission slip.

Their idea of a good read at the pound is a sign posted in big type next to the office door that says: NO ONE IS ALLOWED BEYOND THE PUBIC AREA.

The payment trailer looks like an ice fishing hut decorated by John Nash of *Beautiful Mind*. Although there are four windows for payment transactions, only two were in use the day I was there; and both clerks thought nothing of breaking off to answer phones, catch a cigarette break, or otherwise shoot the breeze with their colleagues in a backroom far from the madding crowd.

A yard worker traipsed in and out of the trailer carrying a thick club. Three women, obviously together, started singing Christmas carols in line while they waited. Their joy suddenly disappeared when a man, seeking to retrieve his truck for the third time, screamed, "Get your supervisor! That's her right there — the one in the grey sweatshirt — she's the one who told me to get the form notarized...All right, then, fuck you. Fuck you all. You can keep the fucking truck."

The pound workers are aided in their sullenness by a management system that seems designed to frustrate both employees and citizens. Claiming your car requires not only a valid driver's license but proof of insurance and registration or title. Fully one in every three drivers at the window keep such documents in their glove compartment — which requires the clerks to issue a temporary yard pass for their retrieval. After getting the documents, drivers then have to return to the same clerk, who photocopies the registration and proof of insurance, separately writes the information on three documents and hand-writes you another yard pass to get your car.

Even then, you are only halfway home. With a new pass in hand, you have to go find your car again (mine was in row 1, slot 135 in a lot that must have stretched back half a mile), drive it up to the gate and return to the same clerk in the trailer to give back the yard pass and hand over your credit card. The window clerk, in turn, carries it to another clerk, then sends you outside again so you can walk around to re-enter a back door, sign the credit card receipt and get your official release slip.

While standing in line (did I mention this whole process took over two hours?) I began to whether we really need a winter parking ban at all. To wit: the Chicago winter parking ban is in effect 120 days a year. How many days during that December to April period does it actually snow here?

According to the Midwest Regional Climate Center in Champaign, which collates National Weather Service data, the snowfall in Chicago exceeded 2" an average of 6 out of the 120 days over the last four years. [Editor note: 1998 – 2002] During the same period, there was an average of 100 days when there was no snow at all.

But still the city towed.

Day in, day out, the city towed. And nicked its poor citizens for $150 towing fees, a $50 ticket and $25 a day in storage fees — a total of $225 — because they parked on a public street that in all likelihood (87.5 percent) had no snow on it at all. What a racket!

It is not a good idea to pursue the idea that a city service is, in fact, a racket—because it just might be.

My thoughts that day at the car pound became an obsession when I learned this October that Mayor Daley has once again awarded the prime city car pound contract to E&R Towing, a Markham-based private towing company that first won favor with the mayor through a politically connected attorney named Martin McNally in 1989.

Originally, E&R Towing was contracted only to remove abandoned cars off city streets and vacant lots — a complaint that rivaled tree trimming atop the list of citizen calls to the mayor's Office of Inquiry and Information.

In 1996, now operating under the name Environmental Auto Recovery, E&R was awarded a 90-day pilot contract for all towing and pound operations at the South Side pound at 103rd and Doty. A year later, it won the first of what would become three successive contracts to tow and operate city pounds on the south side, the west side (703 N. Sacramento) and near south side (4000 S. Ashland). Only the central Loop car pound (under Wacker Drive downtown) and O'Hare Airport remain in city hands, largely because towing there is tightly integrated into police operations.

According to a Streets and Sanitation spokesman, Chicago tows about 200,000 cars a year. Through a highly inefficient system that requires pound workers to tag and input SNOW TOW data into computers, the city estimates about 13,300 of these are snow zone related. If this year's first day haul last Monday is any indication (223 cars), the figure is probably closer to twice that, or 26,000 cars.

In 1998, a Buffalo, N.Y. company named United Road Services purchased E&R as part of a roll up of national towing firms aimed at creating a public stock offering. United Road paid $27 million for the company based on annual revenues of $23 million from E&R operations in Chicago, Aurora, Newark and Avel, New Jersey, according to the *Buffalo Business News.* But the centerpiece of the deal was the Chicago towing contract because E&R controls a network of related companies for scrap iron recycling and/or resale of the abandoned cars that come into its possession.

A skeptic might think the city keeps the winter parking ban because it gets big bucks out of unsuspecting motorists. In fact, Chicago only collects some $20.7 million a year in revenues from all it's towing programs, according to the city budget office, of which some $15.5 million can be tracked directly to cars taken to the E&R operated lots.

An evaluation of the latest city towing contract, however, indicates United Road will receive $12 million of that next year — getting paid $100 apiece for towing 135,000 cars and maintaining the three impoundment lots. The good news is that some 55,000 of those cars will be redeemed by the owners. The bad news is that United Road will, after 90 days, come into possession of the other 80,000 unclaimed vehicles, for which it will pay the city a scrap iron price of $76 per car.

In fairness, most of these are indeed junkers that the city used to pay $100 to haul away. But a *Chicago Tribune* investigation in 1997 found that about 25% — 20,000 cars — are working vehicles that, because of parking tickets or mounting storage fees, go unclaimed at the city lots. Sold for parts, or better yet as used vehicles at nearby auto auctions, they are the gravy in United Road's Thanksgiving, with some going for thousands of dollars over the $76 cost.

Last October, *The Tribune* reported the three losing bidders for the towing contract claimed the bidding procedures were rigged to favor the politically-connected firm. Mayor Daley, as he has in the past, responded that E&R has done an excellent job in cleaning junkers off the street, and turned a money-losing city service into a (small) profit center.

My own review of United Road's bid shows that its proposal was head and shoulders above the competitors — and includes plans to computerize the archaic tracking system. But it's also true the city bid request was tailored to a company with a complete system to tow, store, recycle and re-sell used cars — a qualification only United Road could meet.

The question, of course, is not who got the city towing contract, or why, or whether they charge too much for their services. It's really just a question of whether these snow tows are necessary at all. Why doesn't the city just treat the 107 miles of winter tow zone streets like the other snow routes — where plowing takes place only when snowfall has accumulated to 2 inches?

Because no one can make money that way. And there'd be no place for that cute little snowball named Skippy to go, and nothing for me to think about while I'm standing there — for two hours, did I mention that? — wait-ing to get back my car.

— December 5, 2003

Choosing St. Patrick's Queen

On a cold Sunday in February, with little else to do, I found myself searching out the warm glow of the Plumbers Local 130 union hall on West Washington Street to watch the selection of the next queen of Chicago's St. Patrick's Day Parade.

The contest has been held since 1956 in the plumbers' ballroom, a cavernous Beaux Arts auditorium popular with local politicians. Ninety-five young lasses — most apparently spurred on by mothers, sisters, or aunts who have competed in years gone by — turned out to compete for the coveted title and one of four other spots on the Queen's court.

The criterion for winning is pretty simple. The queen must be a young woman of Irish ancestry, between the ages of 17 and 27, never married, and, in the opinion of the judges, the fairest lass in the land. Determining this last pesky detail is the main purpose of the contest. But, this being Chicago, there are a number of other factors that weigh into the decision.

I arrived at the union hall around noon, unaware that the contest was an all day affair that would not end until dinnertime. The girls — yes, this is one of those affairs where the word is still appropriate — checked in downstairs with their high heels and semi-formal dresses while I joined their parents upstairs in the ballroom.

That is where I found James T. Sullivan, the business manager of Local 130, who proudly explained that the contest, along with pretty much everything else related to the parade, has been the exclusive bailiwick of the Plumbers union since it started. "We provide the marshals. We dye the river green. We do everything," he said.

In the hierarchy of the plumbers union, few jobs are as coveted as being on the crew that dyes the Chicago River green. The task dates back to the era of Sullivan's predecessor, Stephen Bailey, who noticed a young plumber with green all over his hands after applying plumber's paste to a toilet leak. If such a small quantity had that effect, Bailey surmised, it wouldn't take that much more to dye the whole river green, and thus a tradition was born.

Although Sullivan holds the title of general chairman of the parade, the Queen contest bears the indelible stamp of its host Bob Ryan. He is the one who must supply the lively banter that keeps things moving as the field slowly narrows from 95 to 40 to 20 to 5 — and finally The One.

Ryan is a bit of Irish royalty himself, coming from the family of the late Tommie Ryan who marched in the Middle Column of Middle Limerick during the Irish rebellion of 1916. After serving 14 months in prison for his rebellion, Tommie came to Chicago when the 1922 peace treaty was signed and started the Shannon Rovers Irish Pipe Band in 1926. For the next 30 years, he led the Shannon Rovers in the west side St. Patrick's parades. (This was a time when Chicago's south and west side Irish held separate parades.) When Mayor Richard J. Daley was first elected, he asked Tommie Ryan to organize the first "unified" citywide parade in 1956, and a Ryan has been at the center of it ever since.

The Queen contest begins every year with the Shannon Rovers marching down center aisle and splitting to the sides to welcome the 20 judges. Ryan, who has made quite a name for himself as a singer at Irish events, leads the crowd in the singing of two national anthems: Ireland's "The Soldier's Song" and the United States's "Star-Spangled Banner." Then the girls start making their way to the podium, escorted by six tuxedo-clad young lads.

They come to the stage in groups of ten, carrying their contestant number demurely in front of their dresses. On their first pass, they walk, turn and smile, but say nothing. On a second pass, the contestants are asked to step to the microphone to say their name (first names only) and a few words about themselves.

There is no talent contest, no swimsuit competition, no evening gown showcase to help the judges make their decision. There is not even a chance for the contestants to speak out on behalf of world peace. From these brief remarks, the judges will have to eliminate 55 of the would-be queens.

If I were to characterize them as a group, I'd say they are all pretty and all studying to become nurses, teachers or long distance runners. The Catholic high schools of Chicago are well represented, and more girls than you'd expect have already graduated from college and are making their living as marketing consultants for good causes.

My three favorites after the first round (and I was not the only one betting on the outcome) are:

- A waitress attending Elgin Community College who is transferring to Georgetown next year to pursue a degree in International Studies (#14).
- A wedding designer and professional voiceover artist who was just happy to be here (#31).
- An Art Institute graduate and independent TV producer who is competing in her fourth year (#32).

While an Irish dance troupe does a little jigging at the intermission, the judges tally their votes. For a third time, with the field now narrowed to 40, the girls walk to the stage carrying their number. This time, each group of ten is given a few minutes to step down and introduce themselves to the judges. Earlier, Sullivan told me the contest winner was usually chosen based on a mixture of grace, personality and poise. After listening in on a few conversations with the judges, I also wouldn't dismiss the importance of blarney.

Another group of step dancers takes the stage while the judges again winnow the field down. Then, for a fourth time, the girls — still carrying their numbers — walk the center aisle, pose on stage, and have a last chance to charm the judges in one-on-one conversations.

One of the regulars at the annual contest is Mike Houlihan, who used to write the "Houlihan in the Hood" column for *the Sun-Times*. Houlihan has just finished a public television documentary on the contest called *Her Majesty Da Queen* in which he notes that this year's queen almost always comes from last year's court.

The 2009 winner Julie Popp, for instance, served two years in waiting on the court before gaining the crown. Her successor, 2010 Queen Kerry Brennan was Popp's first runner-up the year before.

All of this bodes well for one of my favorites, Sara Collins (#32). She served on the Queen's court for each of the last three years running and was first runner-up to Brennan last year. In the parade program book, she is honored by a full-page ad from "The Collins, The Suglichs, The Doyles, The Mastersons, and Uncle Matt with loving memories of Grandpa Marty."

When Bob Ryan invites the last five girls to the stage to announce the winner, I sneak close to the dais with my little pocket camera to catch Collins' "surprise" at being named the St. Patrick's Day Queen.

Sure enough, Bob Ryan ticks off three finalists who will serve on the court, but not as queen. Collins is one of two left in contention for the honor.

"And our first runner-up is…" Ryan says (inserting the appropriate space for anticipation) "Sara Collins. And our St. Patrick's Day Parade Queen this year is Sarah Goreski."

You cannot grow up Irish in Chicago without knowing in your bones that life is sometimes unfair. Sara Collins had all the attributes of a queen, and she made all the right moves to get selected. Now here she was losing out to a newcomer in the contest, a graduate of LaPorte High School in Indiana and current DePaul University student whose parents live in Norwood Park under a Polish last name.

I was all but ready to call the decision foul when Mike Sneed's column in the *Sun-Times* solved the mystery. Despite the name, Gorecki is Irish to the core. As proof, Sneed noted that her aunt is executive director of the Irish Fellowship Club of Chicago.

And then I understood. It's good to be lucky in Chicago, but better to be connected.

— March 10, 2011

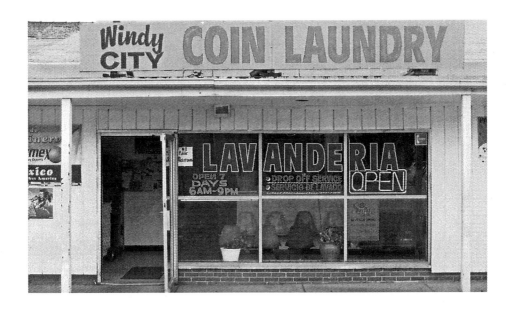

The Laundromats on Fullerton

There are 12 Laundromats on Fullerton Avenue. If you follow them out from Western Avenue to the Brickyard Mall on Chicago's outskirts, that comes to one every three blocks. They have between them 651 washing machines, 749 dryers and several small communities of people devoted to doing our dirty laundry.

Some are almost supermarket size. They hide under colorful signs like Bubbleland, Spin Cycle, Suds, and Scrub-A-Dub that make them seem more like amusement parks than workplaces. Odd corners are filled with kiddie rides, massage chairs, even a gourmet cafeteria. Some feature free Wi-Fi. Others just struggle along, fading reminders that as much as you gussy it up, laundry is a chore silently accomplished, mostly by poor women, out of the mainstream of American commerce.

Laura Garcia, 50, manages the Scrub-A-Dub at 3333 W. Fullerton. It is not an easy life. The Laundromat is open seven days a week (6 AM to 11 PM) every day of the year except Christmas. She splits those hours with two other women in alternating shifts, but she's comfortable in the job, happy with her boss and pleased to have regular customers who appreciate the little extras she provides.

Scrub-A-Dub offers washers at $1.50 — $3.50 (20, 40 and 50 pound loads) and dryers at 25 cents for 15 minutes. The prices vary little up and down the street, so Garcia tries to distinguish her service from the others with supermarket tabloids neatly arranged on the counter, a massage chair, a kid's corner, sandwiches and snacks. The most unusual thing about the job? The sex toys customers drop off with their laundry. "I give it back to them and say 'that's yours to handle,'" she says.

Garcia worked previously as a nurse's aide at a hospital — "That's where I learned to keep things clean" — but started thinking about working in Laundromats when the JM Laundromat opened down the street from her house at Laramie and Fullerton. "They had an attendant named Liz who was really my role model. She made a point of knowing her customers, so I'd only go when she was there."

The JM was the first of the supersized Laundromats on Fullerton and remains the busiest. Liz Milete, Garcia's mentor, was there when it opened eight years ago and still works part-time as general manager. When I arrive, she is busy cleaning up after a washing machine that overflowed. She mops, answers questions and, when that is done, checks in on a picnic table in back where a half dozen kids are wolfing down the donuts she brings in every morning.

"It's always something," she says. "But I like this job. It lets me make a difference." The JM doesn't have the amenities of other establishments on the block, but Milete runs it like a community center.

Besides the free donuts, she brings in books for the kids and reads to them or helps with their homework while their moms are doing laundry. "When I'm not here, I nanny two kids at home. I run the block party in my neighborhood; and I do what I can to fight drugs and gangs there. So when I'm here, I look for ways I can make a difference."

After JM opened, two other supersize laundries launched within two years on both sides, each with its own formula for success. Bubbleland lures its clientele in with cartoon graphics that make it look kid-friendly, and Express Laundry bills itself as Chicago's largest with 132 washers and dryers. It is the only solar-powered Laundromat in the city, and no less a personage than Governor Pat Quinn showed up for the ribbon cutting.

For all the hype, neither is particularly busy on the day I visit. A few kids chase each other around an X-men coin-up ride at Bubbleland; and a freelance DVD salesman roams the empty washers and dryers at Express trying to find bargain hunters. But Milete's concept of community is nowhere to be found.

Not all the laundry owners on Fullerton are happy to see it become the Las Vegas strip of Laundromats. The tattered sign of Windy City Laundry speaks loudly to how hard it is for smaller establishments to keep up (even if its Spanish-speaking owners cannot); and Sue Dwyer, who has run the Surf Laundrette with her husband for 23 years, eyes me suspiciously as I count her washers and dryers.

"You're not going to open another one," she says. "That's what they all do. They count my machines, they check my prices then they open up next door."

Dwyer would like to sell. Her husband is bed-ridden with a lung disease so she runs the Laundromat with the help of her son. The long hours she must stay open keep her away from home, but she knows the chances of someone coming in to buy her out are slim to none. "Nobody buys Laundromats these days," she says.

Except, perhaps, Howard Ha, a Korean, who runs the very busy Spin Cycle laundry at 4418 W. Fullerton. Ha did not intend to buy his laundry. He actually bought a laundry franchise in a chain that was traded on Wall Street. When Wall Street became disenchanted with the business, however, franchise owners were given the option five years ago to buy their store or close.

Ha chose to stay. He knows his customers are 90 percent Mexican and South American. Even in his own establishment, he conducts his business in a closet marked "Employees Only." He leaves customer relations to his Spanish-speaking manager out front. But Ha is a shrewd businessman nonetheless.

He offers a FREE DRY for every washer load over 40 pounds (and makes up for it in the cost of the wash). He leases space in his facility to DolEx, a wire transfer facility that lets customers send money back to families in Mexico. And he quietly watches his income and his customers. "We have so many different characters that come in here," he says. "Sometimes they are bad, sometimes sad, and sometimes they help each other."

Behind twin concrete pillars emblazoned "God Bless America" and "Dios Benedice America," John Shim, another Korean-American, runs the no-frills J & S Laundromat — unless you count the plastic flowers on the window sill as frills.

Shim has no illusions about his customers. "Poor people use Laundromats," he says. Whether they are old Poles, new Hispanics, or the perennial students looking for cheap housing, the two-flat and three-flat apartments in his neighborhood always guaranteed a steady income. "But everything is going condo now," he says. "To sell them, the developers put in washer-dryers. The old customers move away. The minimum wage goes up. The technology gets cheaper. It gets harder to make a profit every year."

After a long day in the Laundromats on Fullerton, I drive home only to notice that I missed one, Brendel's at 2550 W. Fullerton. The sign advertising "Laundromat — FREE WI-FI" is hard to see from the street.

Brendel's is a small, but first class operation. Its motto — "The stamp of excellence" — is posted on every wall. Whose stamp and where it came from is never mentioned.

Iris Correa, the day manager, can't tell me. But she can tell me that Brendel's has been in existence for 38 years. Correa is a pleasant, quiet person. As she talks, I notice above her the posted rules for her establishment:

- No radio playing.
- No kids alone in laundry carts.
- Not responsible for gym shoes in dryer.
- Not responsible for stolen clothes.

A baseball game is in progress on the TV sets. Four or five people quietly do their wash in the darkened, air-conditioned silence. I ask Correa what's different about running a Laundromat today.

"What do you want me to say? It's different these days?" she asks. "It's not. Clothes get dirty and we wash them."

— July 22, 2009

Cans in The Alley

The garbage men come on Thursdays. The homeless come every day in between.

They live at the end of the alley behind the BP gas station. They gather there during the day, their shopping carts pulled to the sides like parapets around their own special fort, living a life only the homeless can understand.

By nightfall they are gone. The lucky ones are back in the shelters, three of them so far in Bucktown, with 900 beds that can be rented for $18 a night. Others you can find sleeping under the Kennedy Expressway beside the Western Avenue viaduct in a sliver of land the city wants to turn into a skateboard park next year.

That's where I found William, a refugee on the streets for the last two years. Two years ago, William was a counselor at the St. Leonard's Rehabilitation Center. Today he is his own man, something of an entrepreneur known as one of the better alley scroungers in the neighborhood.

When I encountered William, he was standing under the viaduct sharing a pint of whiskey and a cigarette with a friend. He stood at the helm of a shopping cart loaded on both sides with trash bags filled with aluminum cans. His prize for the day's hunt—a large metal drum—took up most of the shopping cart proper.

William was headed seven blocks north to the Bucktown Recycling Center, 3041 N. Rockwell, where he will sell his cans for 42 cents a pound unless, of course, they are too contaminated with other garbage.

On a good day, William can make two runs to the recycling center. If he has ten bags of cans on each run — less weight than the average shopper takes to the car from the grocery store — he can get $30 – $40 for each delivery. Add in that heavy metal drum, and he might be looking at a $100 day. From things we routinely throw away.

For as long as she's been in Chicago, my wife has been separating out our empty aluminum cans into a plastic bag and hanging them out in the alley for William and the other shopping cart skippers. She is careful to do it on any day other than garbage pick-up day so the city workers don't toss it in with the regular trash. And never in seven years have I seen a bag hang on our fence for more than two hours.

We do not generate a huge number of empty cans — maybe only two or three pounds a week — but even then, my wife's habit is like taping a dollar bill to the garage door. "Yeah, lots of people do that," William said. "It makes things a lot easier."

At first, I thought my wife was carrying on some hobo tradition she learned from her grandmother in Rockford. Like the pie in the windowsill, the cans on the alley post were some kind of sign that good-hearted people live here. One day, I even returned home to find one of the alley scroungers sweeping up the scattered contents of a blue bag around our garbage cans. "Can you believe it," he said. "Some people just want to mess it up for everyone."

But my wife's practice of hanging cans in the alley, she tells me, arose more out of her anger at the city Blue Bag recycling program than any historical memories. And the more I looked into the program, the more I began to believe she has discovered a far better alternative.

Chicago's Blue Bag recycling program was started in the late 90s when America's cities went on a rampage of urban recycling. According to the National Soft Drink Association, municipal recycling programs were suddenly serving 140 million people — three times the number served in 1990.

Traditional programs require citizens to put cans, bottles and paper into separate containers apart from other waste; these containers are then separately collected and dispatched to recycling centers. The process not only puts a heavy burden on citizens to separate at the kitchen door, but also increases the labor (and trucks) needed to handle the pick-up.

Blue Bag recycling was a Mayor Daley special, another one of those "thinking out of the box" solutions that he would become famous for. Instead of doubling the number of collections, Chicago would ask citizens to put cans, bottles and paper into special plastic blue bags, then toss them into regular cans with the other garbage. At the garbage dumping sub-stations, high tech machinery and a squad of hand-pickers would then pick out the recyclables for separate processing right on site.

The system had inherent inefficiencies and slippage. In theory, what was lost in efficiency would be made up for by the ease-of-use, so the sheer volume of waste processed would yield more recycled material than programs in other cities.

In its first year, the city claimed 34% of the citizens participated. By 2001, that number had slipped to 28 percent. Last January, *The Chicago Tribune* uncovered a city study showing participation has slipped to just 13.3% in 2003. Not one of the 50 city wards has more than a 30% participation rate and some — like the 37th, 20th and 22nd wards — have fewer than 2% of the citizens using the blue bags.

Tribune reporters went with city officials to a South Side waste station to observe the recycling system in action. They saw "a front-end loader flatten 10-foot-high mounds of garbage at the facility on 110th Street." When two workers waded into the pile to pick out the blue bags, virtually none of the few blue bags that dotted the garbage pile were intact.

"The shredded bags were then put into a truck apart from other garbage. As workers carried the bags, recyclables spilled out. One bag yielded a cascade of green bottles, which clanked against the floor and stayed in the mound with the rest of the garbage destined for landfills," *The Tribune* reported. "Shreds of a blue plastic bag were twisted around the arm of the front-end loader, flapping as it moved the garbage around. The loader bucket lifted waste that appeared to include filled blue bags into a dumpster bound for a landfill."

Skepticism about the city's blue bag recycling effort grows. In the city's 19th ward in Beverly, the alderman has convinced the city to undertake a pilot program adopting the suburban-style system for separate pickups of garbage and recyclables. In many north side grocery stores, blue bags for recycling are not even sold. In stores where they are, the cost is almost double that of regular trash bags.

So maybe William and his cohorts behind the shopping carts are showing us a better way, a uniquely American way otherwise known as the private enterprise system. Aluminum is the most profitable material to recycle, and the most environmentally worthwhile because of the latent energy savings in not having to manufacture new aluminum from scratch.

"If ever there was a commodity that begged for recycling, it's aluminum," Allen Hershkowitz, a recycling expert for the National Resources Defense Council, says. Because it takes so much electricity to make aluminum, the latent energy savings in the 760,000 tons of aluminum trashed last year could light up Chicago, Dallas, Detroit, San Francisco and Seattle for a year.

The alley scroungers who pick up our cans in the alley do us a double favor: first by transporting them free to the recycling center, then again by keeping the cans uncontaminated by the other garbage that too often blends into the blue bag contents.

They also receive the highest price for their deliveries because they provide the best quality at the lowest operating cost. (The recycling center will, if you ask, give you a free shopping cart to carry your cans.) The most in-demand recyclable material gets back into the marketplace, and the people who collect it sustain a lifestyle that would otherwise by unsustainable.

There's something quite wonderful about it all. Sad in its own way, but wonderful nonetheless. And so, William, I salute you for your service to the community...and recommend that, next time, everyone put your cans on the fence post in the alley.

— September 5, 2005

Breakfast at Whole Foods

"In my hungry fatigue, and shopping for images, I went into the neon fruit super-market, dreaming of your enumerations."

— *Allen Ginsberg*

To start the year off right, we went to breakfast on New Year's Day at the Whole Foods store in Lincoln Park. Here in the land of yogurt and granola, where progressive thinking is all but a religion, there are all manner of healthful products useful in keeping New Year resolutions. What led me to Whole Foods, however, was not the prospect of a healthier New Year but the more mundane promise of orange juice and a ham and cheese omelet at one of the most talked about new grocery stores in America.

I could have stayed home and concocted breakfast out of the same ingredients in the refrigerator. (This would be in keeping with the one resolution I did make this year: spend less money.) But I had just finished reading about Whole Foods and its enigmatic founder John Mackey in *The New Yorker*; so when my wife mentioned that her friend Connie had taken a job handing out chocolate samples at Whole Foods, I decided to go visit two long lost friends, Connie and the store.

The first Whole Foods I ever went into seemed like a novelty when it opened in Lincoln Park in 1993. It was in a mall next to a transcendental bookstore, and the first thing you noticed at the door was a large display of vitamin supplements. The aisles were stocked with fresh organic products and gourmet food items most grocery store owners couldn't even pronounce. But healthy habits, I discovered, did not come cheap. And it wasn't long before Whole Foods became synonymous with "Whole Paycheck." The extra cost notwithstanding, the concept proved a huge success. A year after the Lincoln Park store opened, the company went public. The Texas-based chain went from three stores to 280, and in May 2009, the old Lincoln Park store closed and Whole Foods opened a new 75,000 square-foot emporium just a block south of the old one at 1550 N. Kingsbury.

Traversing that extra block took me back through 30 years of memories about a no man's land of manufacturing plants that once thrived along the Chicago River's edge. Today, realtors have given that area the trendy name of "SoNo" (South of North Avenue). Back then, it was still in the dark shadow of nearby Cabrini Green, and Kingsbury was a half street— half railroad spur best known as a backdoor shortcut into the Loop — for those brave enough to chance it.

In the early Eighties, the area saw its first new construction in a decade. A gentleman's club named "The Crazy Horse" opened on Kingsbury. Shortly after, a tiny corner tap was taken over by ex-hippies and rechristened "Weeds." One by one, the factory buildings were converted to design studios, media stages, Internet start-ups, and boutique furniture and cabinetry showrooms.

North Avenue blossomed with a string of Pottery Barns, Victoria Secrets, Banana Republics and J Crews. Nightclubs and upscale restaurants settled in next to Weeds. And when the last of the Cabrini Green high rise buildings on Halsted Street came down, the very private (and expensive) British School went up across the street. As if to certify the neighborhood had finally arrived, a developer built a 26-story luxury condo tower smack dab in the middle that opened last year just as the housing bubble was collapsing.

As we neared our destination, we passed three day care centers with trendy names like Chalk, Bubbles Academy and Fantasy Kingdom. (One, I learned later, is so exclusive it has a keycard-protected indoor garage to drop off and pick-up the kids.) It was sad to see that the last of the rail spur customers, Carbit Paints, has a for sale sign on the side, but heartening to note the gentlemen's club is still in business. And just across from it, sprawled out along the bank of the Chicago River, is the magnificent, if awkwardly out of place, Whole Foods.

However dire the economy may be, Whole Foods makes no bones about its desire to be seen as the horn of plenty for a new age. The Lincoln Park store is a behemoth of a grocery, almost the size of one and a half football fields with 420 parking spaces, seven restaurants, two bars, a mezzanine Wi-Fi lounge and a stage for musical entertainment.

In addition to shopping, you can go there for Tai Chi lessons, a chiropractic clinic, a kids *song & story* time every morning, or if you happen to be free on January 23, a celebration of National Yoga Day. At the front door, widescreen TVs pipe a stream of football bowl games to patrons sitting at one bar. Further down, a wine and cheese bar opens later in the day for more civilized mingling (and hook-ups). The aisles are marked by street signs pointing to the "Chicago Bar" (with its 16 spigots of local brews on tap) and "Whole Baby" (an infant aisle featuring chlorine-free diapers) or the "Buy in Bulk" section where, next to the grind-your-own-nut-butter station, you can choose from 21 kinds of nuts, five oatmeals, nine rice grains, and an assortment of other dried fruits and seeds — all arrayed in plastic silos on the wall — to customize your own bag of trail mix.

Walking into the store is like walking into the mouth of a cornucopia. Everywhere is the promise of healthy living, all in abundance. Fruits and vegetables at the entrance give way to a fresh seafood bar, a butcher counter, an enormous beer selection (everything, ironically, except Budweiser and Miller), wines and cheeses from around the world, chocolates, cakes, and any number of exotic petit fours and gelatos. In the yogurt section alone, I counted 21 different brands of yogurt, not varieties, not flavors, but brands, each in an assortment of sizes and calorie counts.

At the Allegro Café, they were featuring a *Celebration Caffe* made of coffee from Costa Rica, Guatemala and Sumatra "with hints of bittersweet chocolate and spice." Not your cup of tea? Then put in your own order with the barista for a custom roast, go shopping and return ten minutes later to pick it up. And speaking of baristas, don't look for Starbucks (ditto Folgers, Maxwell House and Dunkin Donuts) here. The coffee aisle has pretty much everything but.

Although I lingered to look at everything, I put nothing in my basket. Our mission, as I said, was not to shop but to eat. So we pressed on to the dining area where the selection includes Wicker Park Subs, Taylor Street Italian,

Pilsen Taqueria, Asian Express, a Chicago Smokehouse and, my favorite, the Riverview Diner. I ordered the ham and egg omelet with coffee and orange juice. They were no more expensive than at my own neighborhood diner, and quite a bit tastier, although I missed the sass I'm used to getting from the waitress when she brings it. And I ate slowly, savoring the aromas around me, listening to people decide what goes into their shopping basket — and what gets left out.

So I feel now like I'm ready for the New Year. I've caught up with the changes of the last many years, seen the wealth of opportunities for good eating and good living, and demonstrated the self-discipline needed to navigate my way through them without getting carried away. Nevertheless, I didn't want to leave the store without buying something. On my way out, I noticed a crate of coconut water on sale for a mere $2.50 a carton. Reading the label, I learned it is naturally filtered for seven months through the dense fibers of a young green coconut to create a nutritious, pure and refreshing isotonic beverage. It has five essential electrolytes, no fat, no cholesterol, no preservatives, and "more potassium than a banana."

If you work out, drink too much or live on caffeine, you can't get enough of this stuff, according to the label. It regulates your blood pressure and heart function, promotes smoother, healthier skin, and the packaging is BPA-free. Best of all, the product itself is recognized as a winner of the "America's Healthiest" fitness award, and what can be better than that?

I took my coconut water home and poured out a cool one. I think its fair to say: I'm set for the New Year.

— January 6, 2010

Bicycles for Peace

Every afternoon around sundown, I can look out the front window of my Bucktown living room and see a man on a bicycle passing by. He is around 55 years old, slightly overweight, bearded and balding and listening contentedly to headphones as he rides. Depending on the day, he may pass once in one direction and again going the other way. Wondering exactly what route he has chosen through the neighborhood preoccupies my thoughts, but not half so much as my admiration for the bike he rides. It is one of those old fat tire bikes, high handles on the front and a basket on the rear, too new to have belonged to him back in his youth, too old to have come from a store. It is the best of all kinds of bikes — a junker. I want one of those!

If you go south along Western Avenue, you will find in an unmarked warehouse above a car body shop at 927 S. Western the world headquarters of "Bicycles for Peace."

I was directed there in search of a good used bike by a friend who travels in that circle of cyclists that believe no world problem is so great it cannot be solved by fewer cars — or more bikes. Solving world problems was not foremost in my mind, however, when I went down there. Getting in shape was. So my wife and I, and a 12-year-old girl named Sesenia, who has taken us on as her mentors, took advantage of the first warm day of summer to get ourselves outfitted for an urban adventure.

In a flyer that passes around the college campuses every fall, the Bicycles for Peace warehouse is also called The Working Bikes Cooperative. According to the brochure, WBC collects used bikes through the Unity Temple Unitarian Church in Oak Park, refurbishes them in the Western Avenue warehouse and ships them off to third world countries in Africa and South America. In a country like Nicaragua, where the average worker salary is $50/month, a $20 bike in the United States is worth $400 to $500 to its eventual user. The bikes are distributed by a network of priests and social workers, and they have become essential links between home and work for thousands of peasant workers, a keen example of American ingenuity at work.

To defray the costs of repairs and shipping, the public is invited to come down to the warehouse on Wednesdays, Saturdays and Sundays to shop for a "new" used bike. The average price is $25 to $40, but some high tech mountain bikes can run as much as $60 or $100. Still in all, that's hundreds of dollars less than new. Save money and help the poor? What a concept.

Lee Ravenscroft is a tall, scruffy man who does not appreciate customers showing up outside business hours. When we arrived at the warehouse on an off day, only a persistent knocking on the metal door brought him to the window and, I suspect, only the expectant face of Sesenia brought him downstairs to open it. But he was hardly going to accompany us around the place like some store clerk.

"Well, take a look around," he said. "These here are $30 to $50 depending on their condition. The kids bikes are back there." I looked around the warehouse. From one end to the other, crammed into every nook and corner with only a narrow pathway in-between were thousands of bikes! Three-speeds and 10-speeds, mountain bikes, little bikes, big bikes, Barbie bikes, Hulk Hogan bikes. More bikes than you can find in a police stolen property room. They were all there. "Be quick about it. I've got things to do," Lee said.

Sesenia bolted for the backroom like the proverbial kid in a candy store. I lingered around the front trying to decide which bike, exactly, fit my personality. In choosing a bike, I had a few critical needs: a comfortable seat, one that would accommodate my middle-aged ass without doing major damage to my scrotum; handlebars that rose up to meet my hands because, let's face it, I'm not planning to enter the Tour de France; and tires of sufficient fatness they can withstand a Chicago pothole.

The trend these days toward racing and mountain bike designs, aimed at the bicycling enthusiast, ruled out 80 percent of the inventory for me. But I found among them a Schwinn — a recognized name from a fabled Chicago company that went out of business 15 years ago — that was my dream bike as a 13-year-old.

"How about this one?" I asked.

Lee pulled the Schwinn out of the tangle and, flipping it over on its back, spun both wheels and shifted through the gears. "I think we can make this one work," he said.

Meanwhile, Sesenia was scouring the backroom looking for her perfect bike. Sesenia's criteria were much different from mine. She was looking for something of a more current fashion. That ruled out the dozens of high handle-barred, banana seat jobs so popular a few years ago. Accessories were important, but the right color was paramount. Sesenia chose a pink one.

Lee took my bike over to his workshop. A twist on the brake cable here, a wrench adjustment to the seat height there, and I was in business. Sesenia's required a little more work. The front wheel wobbled so Lee used his wrench to unscrew it and replaced it with another.

As he stepped through the process, I marveled at the simplicity of the bicycle. Two wheels, a seat and frame, and a chain strapped around two gears to power it. Braking comes from a handlebar squeeze lever that pinches two rubber pads on the rear wheel. Gears shift through a second lever that slips the chain onto varying sizes of minor gears. In all, there are four adjustable parts — the height of the handlebars and seat, the attachment or detachment of front and rear wheels — all adjustable with a single $2 wrench.

I asked Lee about the origin of the Working Bikes Collective. "It's all volunteers," he said. "We buy these things for $4 or $6 apiece, fix them up and, when there's enough for a shipment, we send them off. We sell what we can here just to make money for the freight, but it works pretty well."

It was only when I asked about their destination that his face lit up. "Bicycles in a developing country can mean the difference between work and unemployment," he said. "In Africa or South America, bikes are used to deliver cargo as well as for transportation. " Since it was started in 2001, Working Bikes has shipped over 1,000 bikes to underdeveloped countries.

"I suppose we could send them Mercedes, but when they break down, how do you fix them? And where do you park a Mercedes in Nicaragua?"

We completed our transaction with the exchange of money: Sixty dollars for my Schwinn — "because it's a classic" — and $25 for Sesenia's pink racer.

Lee was pleased to see us go. "Next time, come during business hours. We have salespeople then."

I am riding my bike these days around the neighborhood, pleased as punch with myself. I bike and stop in the oddest corners of the neighborhood: at a warehouse of imported antique furniture, at ice cream trucks I would otherwise have passed by. I nod at fellow riders along my path and wave at the homeless men gathered under the expressway viaduct. Although I am not carrying cargo or ferrying myself to work, I do believe in some small way, I am riding on behalf of a more peaceful world.

— September 24, 2003

No Love at the Park District

Sarah Eberhard wanted to buy a brick in the new Holstein Park playground that said:

We love you

Adam James

Love, Mom and Dad

After it went through the Chicago Park District lawyers, it said: Adam James.

Andrea and Paul Sill bought a brick in the new Holstein playground that said:

TO A LIMITLESS FUTURE

WE LOVE U

EVAN COOPER

By the time the Park District lawyers got done with it, it read: Sir Evan Cooper.

The Eberhard and Sill families were obviously surprised, but not alone. Of the 50 bricks purchased this year to raise community funds in support of the new Holstein Park playground, ten have been rejected because they don't comply with the Chicago Park District "message policy."

Among the other inscriptions rejected were: ZORRO, WE LOVE YOU (now 'Zorro'); g boutique is a friend of Holstein Park (now 'g boutique/ Holstein Park'); HAVE FUN EVERY DAY, SAM AND NICK (now 'Sam and Nick'); and my favorite: HAPPY FIRST FATHER'S DAY! LOVE, GEORGIA (now 'Georgia'.)

Selling commemorative bricks has been one of the more popular ways local community groups raise private money to underwrite needed playground improvements. But it has also become one of the most convoluted, time-consuming and least profitable schemes in the Park District's fund-raising arsenal.

The problem started in 2002 when Robert and Mildred Tong, responding to an appeal to buy a brick supporting a new Senn Park playground, paid out $50 for a brick saying "Missy, EB & Baby: Jesus is the Cornerstone. Love, Mom & Dad."

Their brick was about to take its place in the park walkway — next to others saying such things as "Bootsie Albert Drennen — Best Cat Ever!" and "We like our names on bricks — Jeff and Julie" — when the Tongs received a letter from Park District general counsel Nelson Brown stating the Park District could not accept any commemorative bricks that have a religious message.

As often happens these days, the Tongs — through the Washington-based Becket Fund for Religious Liberty — filed suit in federal court. In April, 2004, U.S. District Court Judge Ruben Castillo ruled the park district rejection violated the Tong's right of free speech.

"While we recognize the difficulty the Chicago Park District faced in creating substantive guidelines that would provide community members with incentives to donate to buy-a-brick programs," Judge Castillo concluded, "the government cannot broadly invite the public to express something of importance to them and then exclude such an expression because of its religious viewpoint."

Judge Castillo's 28-page opinion went on to criticize the Park District buy-a-brick inscription approval process as incoherent, troublesome and "replete with examples of CPD's confusion. "

The Tongs got their brick, but that's not where the lawsuit ended. Stung by the criticism of its procedures — and aware it needed some more stringent guidelines and review — a group of park district lawyers came up with a new policy in June 2004 allowing donors to put only three things on their bricks:

1) The names of donors or family members (including their titles).
2) The words "in memory of" and a date commemorating a deceased relative.
3) In instances where parks allow pets, the name of the donor's pet.

So while the Tongs won the right to inscribe their brick "Jesus is the Cornerstone" in Senn Park, they are plumb out of luck if they want to buy one just like it this year in Holstein Park. But Bootsie the cat can have all the bricks she wants.

Jessica Faulkner, a Park District spokeswoman, explained that the Park District believes Judge Castillo's ruling came about because there were no consistent buy-a-brick guidelines. Although the Park District has not gone back to the judge for approval, she said the new guidelines, because they are consistent, now allow the Park District to ban such expressions as "We Love You."

The irony of the buy-a-brick dust-up is that the brick program is not all that profitable as a fund-raiser. The cost of purchasing a brick, inscribing it, shipping it to the construction site and installing it comes to around $40. By the time, you add in the architectural design costs of creating a special des ignated area for the fund-raising pavers, the legal time involved in reviewing the brick inscriptions and the administrative costs— rejected inscriptions go from the legal department to the area manager to the park supervisor to the advisory council president (who must tell people to rewrite their brick) — those involved in the process are more frustrated than pleased. And the brick program costs more than it raises.

"When we first heard, my husband was outraged," said Andrea Sill, mother of Evan and a Loop attorney. "I looked at the lawsuit and it seems to me like a humongous overreaction for the Park District to say now that you can't have anything other than a name and a title."

"There are buy-a-brick programs all over the country," she added. "I'm not saying some lawyer doesn't have to be there to say what is acceptable or not. If you've been sued once, you don't want to get sued again. But I'm sure there are models they could follow. They just didn't want to spend any time coming up with real guidelines."

"Then to say our policy is to allow nothing except to list your name —
that's silly," she said. "It kind of defeats the purpose. It certainly takes all
the fun out of it."

— October 14, 2005

Goodbye, Ladies!

For as long as I have lived in Chicago, I have always considered Election Day a holiday. As often as not, I take off work to observe it. I have spent my election days in barbershops, skid row hotels, senior citizen centers and school gymnasiums in all parts of Chicago. I have been a poll watcher and a watcher of poll watchers.

But my most entertaining Election Day experience takes place in my own Bucktown precinct when I walk to the Holstein Park field house to cast my vote in the ladies locker room.

Going to vote is one of the great pleasures I take from being an American. It has almost a tactile feel for me. In the last days leading up to an election, I watch the changing mix of political commercials on TV for late breaking trends. I follow the newspapers a little closer, lend a keener ear to the babble of talk radio and enjoy, among my friends at least, a little bit of a reputation as a political expert. They ask, as they always do, who I think will win. And I tell them, as I always do, I'll let you know on Wednesday.

On Election Day, there's not a lot more any candidate can do to sway voters to his or her cause. So when I wake up that morning, I swear I can hear the birds chirping in the trees. My TV is once again free of political clutter. My front door knob carries Chinese takeout menus again — not the latest political flyer. Never has the expression "it's all over but the voting" been more true. (Except on the telephone, where candidates now robo-call right up to the bitter end.)

I fix myself a good breakfast then I walk to the polls. To get there, I have to walk past my neighbors' houses. Yard signs and window placards proclaim their preferences. Depending on my opinion of my neighbors, I sometimes take their advice or say to myself, "What an idiot."

As I get closer to the park, signs appear hastily stubbed into the ground like little cardboard gardens. Because of the way campaigns are run these days, every candidate seems to have a color. Claypool is green this year, Stroger is red.

If you stand back and look at them collectively, you can tell by the color which way the wind is blowing in your precinct. If you focus in, you may notice signs reminding you of candidates for government jobs—The Cook County Water Reclamation Board?—you never even knew existed. And yet, someone wants my vote enough to plant this seed for me to notice. I'm flattered.

Like most Chicago polling places, we have precinct workers standing out front handing out the Democratic machine's "slate." They are required by law to stand at least 100 feet away, but navigating my way through this cluster of thugs proves the most dangerous part of my journey. They are, for the most part, teamsters, plumbers and members of other unions who work for Ted Lechowicz, the longtime boss of the 30th ward, whose son Ed is running to become a county judge. Lechowicz would like you to believe his son is a key man on the Democratic ticket. The flyers the goons stuff into your hand show a picture of him next to a picture Mayor Daley (who is not even running in this election) and it's hard to miss the inference that Daley couldn't run the city without him. In fact, young Ed is only a few years out of law school. His first job was in the law offices of political fixer Fast Eddie Vrdolyak, and his second is as a legal researcher for the clerk of courts. But he has never argued a case in court, a fact he says shouldn't stand in the way of his deciding them.

Inside the ladies locker room, I can once again celebrate my American democracy. The election judges are a mother I met at a soccer game and an elderly woman I know to be a member of the Bucktown Seniors Club. One is supposed to be a Republican and the other a Democrat, but both were recruited by the alderman, and it probably took a flip of the coin to determine who would be what. One thing they can count on when the polls open is that our precinct captain Jesse Barrera will be there with coffee and donuts to greet them.

Jesse too must stand outside while the voters enter, but he's not just another faceless man in a windbreaker handing out literature. He's from the neighborhood, an old school machine man who sees politics as a way for friends to help out friends. I know because he lives just down the street. On more than one occasion, he's rung my doorbell asking for small favors: a signature on the nominating petition of a friend who is running for state representative; ten dollars for a church raffle ticket; a recommendation for a good eye doctor for an injured city worker (who might need some help with the bills). But he gives as good as he gets: the phone number in the city forestry department of someone who can come out and trim the tree in front of my house; a flyer for a community meeting on the public school lottery system. Once I found him sweeping leaves off my sidewalk and asked him what he was doing. "Just helping out," he said.

When I see him outside the polls, he nods but says nothing. He knows that I know how he wants me to vote. And I know that if I don't—and he loses the precinct—I might be jeopardizing his job. So I scurry past him into the warm comfort of the ladies room. The ballot is long and double-sided. Once I get beyond the four or five top offices, the rest seem like one long string of Irish names vying circuit court sub-districts seats. I vote against any name I recognize. Then I check my hair in the mirror before I leave — the men's room has no mirror — and walk out.

Jesse is all smiles when I emerge. Now that the die has been cast, we can go back to talking again. About baseball. The futility of war. The fools in Washington. All topics we agree on. "Say, did ya hear?" he asks. "They're going to renovate the field house. New boiler, new electric, kids playrooms. You won't have to vote in the ladies room anymore."

"I'll believe it when I see it," I say.

"That's the plan," he says.

I'm not sure how I feel about this change of venue. Voting in the ladies room has been such a leavening experience, proof positive of how egalitarian our democracy is. No one can put on airs in the locker room. But I guess there's no standing in the way of progress.

Goodbye, ladies. Hello, Cookie Monster.

— March 10, 2006

On a Personal Note

Moms & Tots & Me

I'm probably not the first 58-year-old to attend the toddler activities group known as Moms & Tots at Holstein Park. Nannies are regular substitutes and grandmothers have occasionally been roped into the task by their workaholic daughters. But I suspect I am the first man of my age to attend with his 18-month-old son.

The Moms & Tots class takes place every Monday and Wednesday morning in the park playroom where the kids gather to destroy toys, chase around balls and hula hoops, smear finger paints on a table (and themselves), eat a snack, and go home.

My son Nick likes the playroom because they have a plastic kitchen set where he can pull all the plates off the shelves and a padded ramp he can run up and down — practicing for a future career as Sisyphus. They also have cars so big you can climb in and push yourself around with your feet. I like the class because it was the first place I saw him show off.

As our little charges run about, I find myself sitting on miniature chairs with five women I don't know. They are all on a first name basis, with each other and their kids. I can't tell the Natalies from the Ilana's and the Laurens and the Heathers — which ones I'm talking to and which ones are their kids — but they are kind enough to include me in their conversation.

Three of the mothers are pregnant. One has scheduled her delivery for the next day at Prentice Hospital. This prompts a lively discussion of which room she has booked — the corner room overlooking the lake is preferred — and how much better the new Prentice is than the old. I have little to contribute on that front. Yes, I too have been in the new Prentice, but only to visit a friend dying of cancer a couple months ago. I decide to keep that to myself.

There is also a lot of talk about the best museums to visit with your kids. Some like the Kohl Children's Museum in Glenview because it has a great train room. Others prefer the Chicago Children's Museum at Navy Pier, but hate paying for parking.

The gem in this mix of opinion is The Chicago Nature Museum in Lincoln Park and its atrium filled with butterflies. It's got a playful gift shop and plenty of room for stroller parking. "Go on Thursdays. It's free," one says. "Let them run wild in the butterfly exhibit. They'll wear themselves out in an hour so you still have time to get home for the nap."

They call these kids preschoolers because they haven't yet entered the maw of American education. As they progress through life, half the kids who attend public schools in Chicago will never graduate from high school. Less than 20 percent will actually graduate from college. At this early stage of their lives, the sea of writhing bodies before us is all potential. I listen to the moms talk about how they can fill these vessels with cultural enrichment, and I think to myself how much life itself will teach them.

I have two other sons, now 24 and 20, of which I am equally proud, if not more so. They have navigated the shoals of adolescence, gone to college, and come out the other end none the worse for wear. So much of what is good about them has come from finding a career path that interested them, and pursuing it. Dads, I think, are more inclined than moms to give a child his head, to see what he comes up with.

Nick wakes up in the morning with his head bobbing above the crib rail smiling. "Hello," he says, throwing his arms around my neck. I lift him on my shoulder and we open the blinds to look out at the passing cars and trucks on Fullerton Avenue. After we ooh and ah over the things we recognize, we go downstairs for breakfast. I make coffee and a bottle of milk. He eats Cheerios and bananas off the platter of his high chair while I read the *New York Times*.

My wife comes down (no later than 7 AM) and asks whether I fed him breakfast. I say yes. Then she makes him a "real" breakfast and I go off to work.

Being a father again, with two other grown sons, gives you a certain perspective on child rearing you won't find in all the books and websites devoted to the topic. Stuff happens. The child development specialists don't tell you that in the advice they dispense.

You can get weekly emails these days telling you what kind of behavior to expect at each stage of your child's development, when his teeth will come in, when he will throw his first tantrum, and how to say no. But that never really prepares you for the subtle ways that stuff happens.

You can organize play groups to help your child socialize, debate whether Suzuki violin is more beneficial than Wiggleworms, and buy all the Baby Einstein DVD's you want. Kids inherently have minds of their own. I have never seen my son more creatively engaged than when he is emptying out a kitchen drawer.

All I can tell you as the voice of experience is that you can't plan the kid's future. You can give him opportunities, but you have to recognize that sometimes he won't take them. As proud as I am of my son's newfound ability to run up and down a ramp, I know it is a passing phase. He's a healthy, curious and adventuresome kid. He'll master tasks and move on. He'll play with cars, then someday, perhaps, build them. Or maybe he'll write poems about them. Stuff happens.

The only advice I have to my fellow moms is chill out. Growth takes time. Pay attention to all the warning signs of a medical problem, but don't think every failure to achieve is a sign of a learning disability. You can't doctor your way out of who your kid was born to be. You can only encourage them along the way to find that out for themselves.

— February 27, 2009

Potty Boot Camp

I have just come off the experience of spending a weekend locked in the house with a naked 3-year-old and a dying dog for potty boot camp. I recommend you try to avoid it, if you can.

The dog defecated anywhere she chose. After 12 years, with a tumor the size of a grapefruit attached to her liver, Gracie knew what was expected of her. She just couldn't help it. My son was a different matter.

When I was raising my first two boys, the reigning child psychologist of the day was T. Berry Brazelton, who counseled that the child will tell you when he is ready to go to the potty. My memory of their efforts is hazy. (After all, it was 20 years ago.) As I recall, however, it was a long, slow process of trial and error.

Today, patience in potty training is no longer a virtue. A generational shift in child rearing is now tilting toward the theories of Dr. Suzanne Riffel, a self-described "eye doctor and mom," who claims potty training can be done in a weekend if you follow the simple rules she lays forth in Potty Boot Camp.

Scientific studies give conflicting data on when is the best age to potty train: 18 months, 2 years, 3–4 years, whenever. Some studies say it doesn't matter. Some claim potty training is linked to a child's future success. But who are we kidding? What does anybody remember about their own potty training?

What is not in dispute is that the sooner a child learns to pee and poop in the potty, the more ready he or she is to go out into the world on his own. The first of these adventures used to be kindergarten. But the explosion of pre-school programs has lowered the threshold from 5 to 3 years — and no one is more of a potty Nazi than a pre-school teacher. (Some schools even have a "three strikes and you're out" policy.) So the pressure was on my wife and I to bring young Nick up to speed. Six months ago, my wife purchased a Fisher Price Royal Potty in a Box that rang out a triumphant greeting when a child peed or pooped onto its electronic sensors. I made fun of it at the time; but in the spirit of whatever works, I hauled it out and put it in front of the TV.

Our plan was to follow Dr. Riffel's 11-step program. This is also known as the "naked and 75 dollar" method: naked because the child goes the weekend without diapers and $75 because that's the cost of cleaning up the mess.

The eleven steps Dr. Riffel recommends in Potty Boot Camp are:

1. Take the child to the potty. Pull down his pants. Make him sit for 5 minutes.

2. Be cheerful. Make a game of it.

3. Set timer for 10 minutes.

4. Give the child liquids to drink.

5. When the timer goes off, check child's pants. If dry, applaud, clap or cheer.

6. Make him sit on potty again for 5 minutes.

7. If no pee or poop, return to Step #3.

8. Accident? This is what President Obama would call a teaching moment. "Calmly but firmly talk about how pee and poop go in the potty and not in their pants...Perform cleanup procedure (see Appendix A).

9. Drill time. "Explain to the child that they now have to practice going to the potty." Walk to another room then walk briskly back to the potty..."all the while talking about needing to practice since they had an accident."

10. Do this 10 times. Be firm. Do it even with crying or complaining.

11. Go back to Step #3.

Sounds simple, right? And if you follow the program, Dr. Riffel claims that 90 percent of potty training can be accomplished in two days. I went to sleep Friday night dreaming of never having to change a diaper again.

I'd become accustomed to my son sleeping until 6 AM. Saturday morning, I opened one eye in bed at 5:30 and found him staring in my face. He had a big, angelic smile on his face.

"Hello," he said, "I want SpongeBob."

Dr. Riffel warns that TV is a reward that should be withheld for good performance. I was never good at following instructions. We trundled downstairs. I flipped on the TV. I made coffee and read the morning newspapers on the front stoop. Then I changed his diaper, but deliberately did not replace it.

When my wife came down to make breakfast, I noticed that my son, with an embarrassed grimace on his face, was tinkling on the floor. I scooped him up and raced over to the Fisher Price toilet. "Here is where you tinkle," I said. To my son, the Fisher-Price toilet was as good a place as any to watch TV. But my wife insisted we follow the rules so she set the timer — and spent the rest of the day watching and waiting (repeating steps 1 to 3).

It was almost 4 o'clock in the afternoon before we heard the first electronic music alert us that our son had peed. We rushed over and lifted the lid to find a quarter cup of tinkle. High fives all around!

"Way to go," my wife said. "What do we do next?"

"Give him a reward," I said.

"What kind of reward?" she asked.

"I want an Oreo," he said, as if this were an open debate.

"Give him an Oreo. He's the man! He deserves it," I said.

"We can't give him an Oreo every time he goes to the potty. That's too much sugar," she said.

"Life has its trade-offs," I said.

Saturday night in the crib without a diaper was a disaster. Poop and pee everywhere. Dr. Riffel counsels that there are worse things than for a child to feel the icky stuff ooze down his legs without a diaper — or to understand that he has fouled his own nest.

For whatever reason — and I maintain it was the Oreos — my son peed three times in the potty Sunday morning. I rewarded him each time with an Oreo cookie. He became used to saying, "I did it." And I became used to saying, "Here's your Oreo."

That Sunday my wife went on a grocery shopping expedition and found mini-Oreos that satisfied his need for a treat without sacrificing her aversion to sugar. He continued peeing on schedule, but the reward was apparently not enough to get him to poop so we upped the ante. Big Oreos versus small Oreos was my idea. If he peed, he'd get a small Oreo. If he pooped, he got a big one. Never underestimate how important it is for a boy to have the biggest Oreo on the block.

After Boot Camp weekend, my wife and I went back to work. Our nanny was left with the burden of carrying on potty training in a world of summer camps, visits to the pool, and riding tricycles with his friends on the sidewalk in front of our house. More than once he had an accident. It seems easy for boys to know when they need to pee, but harder to admit they want to poop. Poop for boys, apparently, is a concept that's hard to get your head around. Our nanny thought he almost had it one day when he woke up from his nap saying he wanted to go to the potty. He plopped a ripe turd in the toilet. But when she saw a trail of excrement leading back to his crib she knew it was an afterthought.

The next day, my son told her he had to go to the potty again. She rushed him inside the house and, sure enough, the Fisher Price Royal Potty in Box heralded the arrival of excrement.

"You get an Oreo," she said.

"I need a big one," he said.

I can't say we've crossed the Rubicon of the River Shit. But we're handing out big and little Oreos these days like they're free play coins at Chuckie Cheese. We haven't used a diaper since the first day we undertook Potty Boot Camp. And we've only done damage to about $15 worth of kiddie underwear — so far.

I guess it just goes to show: Knowing where to put your own shit — down the toilet — is the first sign of growing up.

— August 19, 2010

The Health Benefits of Jell-O

The popularity of The South Beach Diet has brought into high relief the health benefits of Jell-O — a staple in the South Beach dessert category — mainly because it has no health benefits at all.

The primary benefit of Jell-O in any dieter's regimen is that it is easy to make, can be eaten with a spoon and serves as the approximate equivalent of food. Today's "sugar free" versions on the store shelves boast they have only 10 calories per serving. That's 1/200th of the recommended daily calorie requirement. So if you like it, go ahead, have two.

In real terms, Jell-O is a food substitute made out of two cups of water, into which is poured a packet of gelatin that after four hours of refrigeration will provide four servings of pure food placebo to the hungriest dieter in America. As anyone even vaguely aware of food advertising knows, "There's always room for Jell-O."

Well, duh! If you read the package, Jell-O provides 0% of the minimum daily requirement for fat, protein, carbohydrates and fiber. So gorge yourself on it! We're talking about eating congealed flavored water (and even the flavor is artificial). The more you eat, the less it matters. It has no nutritional value.

In one of those new media marketing deals where process and product become as one, the author of the South Beach Diet has allowed Kraft Foods to advertise that Jell-O is "South Beach Diet Recommended." The endorsement has made Jell-O the hottest thing in the supermarket since sliced bread. (Hotter, actually, because bread is not recommended at all.)

Last Christmas, my sister-in-law, knowing my culinary prowess in the kitchen, gave me a book call "The Magic of Jell-O" with 100 recipes for Jell-O concoctions honoring the 100 years that Jell-O has been a marketed food brand.

After my wife put me on the South Beach Diet — let me put that differently — after I asked my wife to let me participate in regulating my calorie intake, I pulled out the Jell-O book looking for a few good recipes.

The Lemon Charlotte with Raspberry Sauce, Pear Terrine and Cappuccino Cups seemed like a good compromise with the requirements of South Beach. So I went out to the grocery store to get the ingredients.

"Take it back," my wife said. I was still unpacking the groceries, but a couple dozen boxes of Jell-O were out in clear sight on the table.

"What's the matter? I got the diet Cool Whip and the half-and-half is skim, and the rest is just fruit," I said.

"The Jell-O is not sugar free. It's out of regulation," she said.

I would have known that if I'd actually read the South Beach Diet book — or maybe called the Jell-O Hotline (1-800-431-1001) — before I ran off like I was some Jell-O Julia Child. I know better now.

I also know after a little more research that if I am ever passing through LeRoy, New York, I will be stopping at the Jell-O Museum to learn more about this remarkable product. While I'm there, I will look in on the art gallery to see tributes to Jell-O drawn by such American artists as Maxwell Parrish and Norman Rockwell; gaze upon pictures of the original 1904 Jell-O Girl and others through the ages; and listen to Jack Benny first sing the "J-E-L-L-O!" jingle on his 1934 radio show.

My own history with Jell-O doesn't go that far back. But I do recall eating more than my share of shredded carrots chilled in orange goop as a child and finding in my mother's kitchen an incomprehensible array of Jell-O molds shaped like bunnies, hearts, goblins and turkeys.

Now that I am a South Beach Dieter, I find my Jell-O intake is coming in little Tupperware cups. I take them to work on the days when I get tired of eating a cheese stick snack. I have eaten all four original flavors — orange, lemon, strawberry and raspberry — plus lime (introduced in 1930) and, my favorite, a black cherry version introduced as part of the sugar free line.

"So what happens when we get tired of Jell-O?" I asked my wife the other day. "Do we just start drinking Kool-Aid?"

"If it's artificially flavored, and made with enough Splenda…that sounds really good," she said.

—April 1, 2005

Shoe Shopping With Men

If you ever go shoe shopping with men, here's a tip: don't plan on staying long. For a man, there are really only two questions when shoe shopping, black or brown, ties or loafers? And underlying those, a more central one: *why* can't I just wear my gym shoes?

I have a friend who is fond of the expression, "Shoes make the man." He claims he can tell where the power in the room lies simply by looking at people's feet. Anyone can wear a suit, he says. Even the store clerks at Men's Wearhouse have a pretty sophisticated eye toward what cut best fits a man. But for most men, shoes are an afterthought (if a thought at all). The man who takes the time to match shoes to clothing has thought through the presentation process. He's a man on the go.

A sharply shined dress shoe is the ultimate mark of distinction, according to my friend. Although he prefers the modest anonymity of black or brown, he has been seen on rare occasions sporting beige moccasins with his casual wear, or white patent leather shoes with a white suit. Both are blatant calls for attention, he admits, while gym shoes, often deemed an act of rebellion, are more likely a sign the guy is clueless about his own appearance.

My friend gives extra points to a gentleman who makes sure his shoes are shined before leaving the house. I have to believe that is a holdover from his days as a traveling salesman when there wasn't much else to do in his motel room. I haven't noticed any great run on the shoe polish shelf at the grocery store lately (Do they still carry shoe polish?) and I'd be hard pressed to even find a tin around the house.

When I see someone with a shine on their shoes, I figure it is part of the waterproofing solvent they put on at the factory.

Then again, I'll never be mistaken for the power in the room. My approach to footwear is to buy one pair of "good shoes" and wear them for all occasions. (Except in the summer when I try to get away with sandals and no socks.) I know that everyday use can be hard on a shoe — especially in the winter if you tromp through the snow without boots — but as long as they keep out the water and the holes don't show on top, I'll wear those shoes until the bottoms drop off.

And how do you know a shoe is worn out? When you wake up one morning and say, "Honey, where are my shoes?" And she replies, "I threw them out."

It was on just such a morning that I went out shoe shopping with my wife at the local Payless shoe store. I don't have any qualms about going to Payless. (I grew up next door to the Paylesses, and they always seemed like very nice people.) The one nearest my home sits in a mall between a Petsmart and an appliance store, and its windows are always plastered over with sale posters. The day I went, the bargain of the day was 50 percent off on sandals.

What you immediately notice on entering a Payless is they know their customer. There are seven aisles of shoes on display — six of them devoted to women's and children's sizes. The men's department is a single aisle where shoes are displayed in open boxes by size. In my size, the selection consists of two kinds of sandals, three dress shoes (two black, one brown) and a small assortment of moccasins and hiking boots. I picked out my dress shoes (black, no laces) in less than a minute. While we were there, my wife suggested that I also get a pair of sandals. I picked one and was ready to go.

"Aren't you going to try them on?" she asked. I set the boxes down, slipped on the sandals and walked the full 20 feet up and down the aisle. "Like wading in mud," I proclaimed. "Let's go." I took my two purchases to the cash register. The clerk tallied the bill: $60. The whole episode took about eight minutes.

"You call that a shopping experience?" my wife sniffed. "You need to make choices to go shopping. We could have done that on the Internet."

I have no doubt my new shoes were lovingly crafted in China, although Payless goes to great lengths to disguise it. The dress shoes are sold under the State Street brand and the sandals carry an unreadable logo of initials easily mistaken for "REI." Both are a testament to how far form-fitted rubber molding has come in the last few years.

Upon close inspection, my new dress shoes consist of three pieces of leather (or a leather-like synthetic) attached to a hard rubber platform otherwise known as the sole. Indentations along the edges imply that the casing of the shoe has been stitched to the sole, but they are just that — indentations pressed into the rubber at the factory to resemble a stitch line.

These are not shoes you are going to wear for a couple years, then take back to the cobbler to be re-soled with a fresh heel or leather sole. Over time, the rubber will just wear down around the edges. The adhesive holding the leather to the sole will crack. The factory shine will wear off. And one day you'll wake in the morning saying, "Honey, where are my shoes?"

— July 14, 2011

Water, Water Everywhere

There's a great upheaval in the neighborhood this summer. Our grocery store has been re-designed to become a Dominick's Superstore. This is in response to the decision by big box retailers like Target and Walmart to carry non-perishable grocery items, but it also has come about because computer-based checkout registers are yielding an ever more complex array of data on not only what we buy, but how we shop.

When I enter my Dominick's, a server now greets me with an offer of a sample Green Tea Frappuccino from the nearby Starbucks counter. Instead of running my cart up and down the aisles, I'm invited to stroll through a French market of flowers, fresh fruits, vegetables and delicatessen delights, then take a lap on the boulevard of high prices that circumnavigates the store.

For months, store employees have been re-arranging items on the shelves to achieve this new look. Canned goods, cereals, staples, and other low margin groceries are tucked into the center aisles so now, instead of meandering up and down the maze of aisles, I skirt along the perimeter, leaving my cart only to dart in and out to get what I need. One thing that has not changed is the liquor department's exalted position at the end of my journey. Tired of shopping? Grab a six-pack and reward yourself for a job well done.

No, wait a minute. Don't run to the liquor so fast because this week I discovered one last wrinkle in the plan: water. Rows and rows of bottled water, ranging in price from the store brand at a penny an ounce to imports from

England and the Italian Alps that can cost up to 12 cents an ounce (about double the price of beer).

Think about it. If you were buying this stuff from a pump at a gas station, it would be costing you $15 a gallon. You don't have to do that though. You can, if you want, just turn on the tap and get all the water you want free. But who does that? Fewer and fewer of us.

Since 1980, the annual per capita consumption of bottled water in America has grown from 3 gallons a person to 26 gallons, a sizable enough jump to interest even the biggest food conglomerates. Perrier is credited with opening the American market to bottled water in the 1970s and another European import, Evian, made water a supermarket staple in the 1990s. To compete, Pepsi launched its Aquafina brand in 1997 and Coke quickly responded with its own water brand called Dasani. Fittingly enough, they are now the #1 and #2 bestsellers in the country.

But the floodgates, so to speak, are now open to other competitors, including generic water from the grocery chains themselves. Walt Boyes, a consultant in water treatment and distribution, recently told brandchannel. com that anybody with a $100,000 bottling machine can get in the business. "If a store can make its own water in its distribution center for 10 cents a bottle and sell it for $1.25 a bottle, they'll make more money than if they are selling a name brand at a three percent margin."

Since water is water, competing brands only have a few ways to differentiate themselves: namely the purity of the source, the shape of the bottle or the mythic history of the company. Dominick's makes only a feint at creating a brand by calling its generic product "Refreshe" with an extra e. Others have invested more heavily in their image.

Paraviso Qvaszia, an Italian import that costs 8 cents an ounce, arrives from the Italian Alps near Lake Como in a pyramid-shaped bottle "visually pleasing on any table setting." Jana's Skinny Water (also 8 cents an ounce) doesn't have much of a bottle to look at, but it is said to come from artesian wells in a little town in Croatia — and is enhanced with a diet-suppressant they call CitriMax.

Bottlers TAU and Ty Nant (both 11 cents an ounce) also have spectacular bottles and water from Bethania, Wales, in the United Kingdom.

My personal favorite is Smartwater ($2.15 per bottle or 6.4 cents an ounce). It comes with a little story — in really hard-to-read small type — on the bottle:

"Is it just us or do clouds get a bad rap? While we admit they're not as great to have around on a beach day, as say, the sun, clouds are unsung heroes because they contain nature's purest source of water. Meanwhile, spring water comes from the ground and contains random stuff and whatever else the animals that swim in it leave behind. That's why we copied our white puffy friends by creating Smartwater. It's vapor distilled so it is in its purest original state. It's a difference you can taste...unless, of course, you have no taste buds (then you're on your own). But, we don't stop there. We one-up the clouds by adding electrolytes just in case you do decide to hit the beach. Unfortunately, we can't fix the whole men with hairy backs thing."

Now that's a sales message that's going to bring in a lot of smart people.

I'm not sure why I'm telling you all this. It's a slow week in the doldrums of August so what better time to contemplate our fascination with buying expensive water?

When I wheel my cart past the liquor department to the checkout counter, I think maybe I should write Augie Busch a letter on how to double Budweiser's profits. Skip the malt. Forget the hops. Throw away the fermenting formula. Dump the beer. Sell the water.

— Aug 25, 2006

Waiting for Michelangelo

I'm sitting here surrounded by 120 CD's of the music that once defined my life. There's Dylan and Springsteen, The Beatles, The Stones, The Eagles, The Byrds — you can see where this is going, it's a nostalgia-heavy collection — and there's no greater proof than the fact this collection has been sitting in my office closet for 10 years, maybe more, in sealed boxes.

Next to the CD's is a box of old newspaper clippings, cartoons, phone lists and rejection letters from publishers; beside it, a second box of what can only be described as trinkets — snow globes, bobble-head dolls, a sumo wrestler fan, a statue of Albert Einstein and a singing frog my son bought me on a vacation in Puerto Rico.

All this collects around my desk chair because, more than a decade after buying this house, I am waiting for Michelangelo to come paint my office.

Michelangelo is not the maestro of office painting his name implies. He is a house contractor my wife met at Home Depot in the depths of despair over not marrying a handyman. His real name is Michael Angelo, but for the purpose of picking up handyman jobs at the hardware store, he is happy to embrace the confusion.

I myself would not have considered using his services until a recent hailstorm brought home the fact our house is getting old. Obviously, we needed some professional assistance so we invited Michelangelo over for an estimate. Water seeping through the roof combined with general settling created a crack in the living room wall that required both a plaster and paint job — Michelangelo's specialty — but, as we all know, you can't just paint one wall, or even one room.

My wife and Michelangelo agreed the whole question of how the color scheme flows into the dining area, not to mention the stairwell where my 4-year-old son last winter fashioned an abstract mural out of permanent ink marker, required a global approach to redecorating. Plus there were all those nicked corners and loose doorknobs that have gone unattended all these years. They walked through the house attending to each little flaw. When they returned to the living room, Michelangelo had a list of needed improvements a page long.

"And what about your office?" he asked, poking his head into my cubbyhole.

"I'm fine here," I said.

"But have you ever seen your office in white?" he asked.

Okay, I admit that there are water stains in one corner and whole sections of office wall where the paint is peeling off. But the yellow tinge to the walls? I prefer to call it ochre, or the subtle glow cast by my vintage lamp (with the low wattage bulb) designed to bring a creative calm to the room.

As a workplace — a place where you an actually get some work done — my office is a model of efficiency. Side by side desks give me a large surface area for my computer and printer, a charging station for my cell phone, two glasses filled with pens, a stack of yellow pads and an endless supply of printer paper (which I keep on the floor). And those walls, well they function as sort of a 360-degree bulletin board for all the little things you'd hate to just throw away.

Important papers I keep in an old file cabinet in the corner. Mortgage documents, car insurance, software disks and manuals — all the things you'll never need until you need them — are stored there. For everything else, I use the Socratic piling system, stacking papers in the order that they come to my attention until one pile falls into another and I can't remember why I kept them in the first place.

It was easy enough for Michelangelo to boast he could paint my office in a day. "We'll just move everything into the center and have it back before you get home," he said. And much as I wouldn't mind seeing what my office would look like with white walls, he kept overlooking one hard fact: I didn't *want* to move all that junk.

Last week I acceded to my wife's demands and began packing my stuff. You'd be surprised how easy it is to fill a dumpster with your past. Old cameras, computers and cell phones...gone. Along with them, cables and cords with connectors that no longer match up to anything. Accordion files filled with notes for old stories and books. Who needs them? Goodbye rough drafts of screenplays no one will produce and overstock copies of books nobody bought.

A friend of mine recently had to clean out the house of his father, a retired journalist, after his death. "Writers are the worst," he said. "They save everything." I tried to explain why it's necessary to save everything, for reference, because you are always rewriting. But that makes no sense if you are dead. So out went the drafts...and notes for stories I meant to write but never got around to...and stories I wrote that nobody wanted to publish.

Not everything found its way to the dumpster. I put aside a manila envelope to hold photos, letters and a few other pieces of correspondence that somehow felt historically significant. I labeled it "Docuwall" and stuck it in the "deep storage" file cabinet.

I also started a new pile of "things I have that someone else might need." Then I started matching those items up to people who might want them — and was sorely disappointed. "I used to do something like that," another friend told me. "When I cleaned my room, I used to gather up all the stuff I didn't want and put it on my little sister's bed. 'Here's a present for you,' I told her. She was not impressed."

There is one more step in the clean out process that may be the most time-consuming. Remember those CD's? (How long are *they* going to be around?) I spent an evening loading them into iTunes, picking and choosing among my favorites from each album. Then I systematically began scanning old photos (and my children's art work) into the iPhoto library on my Mac. The bulk of the physical material is now gone, but one basic problem remains. Just as you can never just paint one room, you can't move things from one storage device (the walls) to another (computer) without creating a structure for finding it.

So I spend another day creating folders for various items and trying to come up with names that I won't forget 13 years from now. I don't think all of this has made my life any more organized, but it feels good that it is now tucked away in digital bits. And I can't wait until a few years down the road when I can upload those files again to my office in the cloud, where they promise I will never have to paint the walls again.

— July 6, 2011

Uneven Sidewalks

We are living today in the aftermath of a heavy storm.

Outside my front door, six inches of snow greet me this morning. As I step gingerly into the fluff (in slippers) to retrieve my morning paper, I say to myself "This will have to be shoveled." Will I do it myself, or wait for a kid on the block to come by to do it for me (and cash)?

Sidewalks in a city of Chicago's size are pedestrian pathways designed to keep people out of the streets. In the winter, sidewalks give pedestrians the edge because the side streets, especially those that don't carry commuters through neighborhoods, rarely get plowed.

In recognition of the importance of keeping the walkways open in winter — if only to get down to the corner store for milk and diapers — Chicago imposes a $50 fine on homeowners who do not "create a proper pathway" in front of their home. The ordinance is rarely enforced, but sets a tone for civic responsibility that homeowners are expected to take seriously.

On my block, the 2300 block of Medill Avenue in Bucktown, I walk every day down to Pepe's and marvel at the pathways my neighbors have cleared.

Some are large and wide, an edge-to-edge sweeping of snow off the concrete. Others are no more than a pathway, a shovel-wide acceptance of civic responsibility. A few, but only a few, are not shoveled at all.

In the shovel ways in front of their houses, I judge my neighbors. I know one is 78 years old and retired, but he is the first to shovel. The bank executive down the street is out of town, so I excuse his malfeasance. A neighbor down the way has just bought a snowblower, so I applaud his exuberance in clearing his — and both his neighbors' — sidewalks.

But as I look at the overall pattern of sidewalk clearing in the snow, I see tidiness next to sloth, exuberance and isolation knitted together into a mosaic of the citizenry. And somehow it all works because somehow, every time it snows, there is a pathway to the corner.

In the uneven clearing of sidewalk snow, we discover little things about our neighbors, and ourselves, that stay with us throughout the year. Our paths are all connected.

— February 13, 2004